BUDAPEST EXIT

BUDAPEST EXIT

A MEMOIR OF FASCISM, COMMUNISM, AND FREEDOM

Csaba Teglas

Texas A&M University Press
College Station

The paper used in this book meets the minimum requirements
of the American National Standard for Permanence
of Paper for Printed Library Materials, Z39.48-1984.
Binding materials have been chosen for durability.

Drawings on pages 40, 60, 70, 78, 108, 122, 132, 138, and 144
are by Lajos Szalay.
Drawings on pages 6, 10, 26, 52, 128, 150, and the cover are by Lajos Szalay and are reprinted
by permission of Herman Ottó Museum, Miskolc, Hungary.

Lajos Szalay, born in Miskolc, Hungary, in 1909, attended the Hungarian Academy of Fine
Arts, and refined his talents while living in Paris, Argentina, and New York. He is best known
for his expressive monochrome drawings and book illustrations, particularly those concerned
with the Hungarian Revolution of 1956. In 1988, Szalay returned to Hungary to live and do-
nated 450 of his drawings to the Ministry of Culture and several Hungarian museums.
He died in his free homeland soon afterward.

Library of Congress Cataloging-in-Publication Data
Teglas, Csaba, 1930 –
    Budapest exit : a memoir of fascism, communism, and freedom /
Csaba Teglas.
    p.   cm. —— (Eastern European studies ; no. 7)
ISBN 0 - 89096 - 823 - 3
        1. Teglas, Csaba, 1930 –   .   2. Hungarian Americans — Biography.
3. Refugees, Political — United States — Biography.   4. World War,
1939–1945 — Personal narratives, Hungarian.   5. Fascism — Hungary.
6. Communism — Hungary.   7. Hungary — History — Revolution, 1956 —
Personal narratives.   I. Title.   II. Series: Eastern European
studies (College Station, Tex.) ; no. 7.
E184.H95T43   1998
943.905'2 — dc21
    [B]   97-46671
                                                                      CIP

CONTENTS

ILLUSTRATIONS

SERIES EDITOR'S STATEMENT

In the present *fin de siècle,* one can detect a tendency for what used to be bona fide autobiographies to become, vis-à-vis the cultural expectations of the postmodern times in which we live, both autobiographies *and* social analyses. This is precisely what Csaba Teglas's *Budapest Exit: A Memoir of Fascism, Communism, and Freedom* achieves: On the one hand, he offers a readable, personal, and emotionally endearing account of his life through the communist era in Hungary. It is as if he is writing it for his grandchildren, in a style that makes it seem more credible for the rest of us. On the other hand, and despite the lack of formal sociological training, he presents a vivid, contextual, social analysis that transforms—via the sociological imagination described by C. Wright Mills—his personal troubles into the generalized troubles of a large group of people who shared his suffering. Mills called for this sort of social analysis way back in 1959. It is finally becoming fashionable. Nor should Teglas's lack of formal sociological training be used against him: As the eminent social scientist David Riesman has remarked on numerous occasions, the best sociologists in this century have been amateurs.

So why is Teglas's study significant and what can we learn from it? First, it points to a relative neglect by Westerners for understanding the human tragedies and suffering caused by communism. The horrors caused by the Nazis have been documented by Elie Wiesel and others much more frequently than the evils of communism. To be sure, the Cold War led to plenty of ideological analyses of communism, but relatively few analyses of the human suffering it caused. Teglas reminds us that Stalin was every bit as monstrous as Hitler. I hope that his story will inspire other survivors of communism, those from Poland and the Czech Republic to Montenegro and Albania, to finally tell their stories.

Second, Teglas's account demonstrates what was once considered unthinkable: that communist totalitarianism and "brainwashing" often did *not* succeed in breaking the spirit of its victims. It is clear that Teglas and others found ways to form small groups and communities that resisted that ideology, and it is fascinating to read his accounts of *how* they pulled this off, with Big Brother watching nearly all the time, and with the constant danger of someone anonymously turning them in. One hopes that something similar will be possible in countries that are still communist, such as China, North Korea, and Cuba.

This account also shows how informal organizations and non-government small groups were willing to help the refugees who escaped through the Iron Curtain, while the United States and Western Europe were all too willing to ignore Eastern Europe. Governments could have done more, then as now (in Bosnia), to come to the aid of victims of oppressive and imperialist governments. And one wonders how and why the generosity of so many people who helped the refugees in the 1950s seems to have shriveled into what is now commonly called "compassion fatigue."

Finally, *Budapest Exit* demonstrates that history keeps repeating itself and that humanity seems to learn very little from its past mistakes. I agree with Teglas's allusion to the similarity of his condition in communist Hungary and the state of so many victims in present-day Bosnia-Herzegovina. The West still resorts to appeasement when confronted with government-sponsored brutality. And as for the possibility of escape, it seems that ways of escape are increasingly more difficult to find. These are among the thought-provoking and sobering lessons to be found in this moving book.

—Stjepan G. Meštrović
SERIES EDITOR

BUDAPEST EXIT

INTRODUCTION

"Dad, tell us again about your escape through the Iron Curtain," urged Nicholas, my older son, when he was about twelve years old.

"No, no, I want to hear about when you played chess with the Russian captain during the war," demanded Gordon, my younger one.

Such requests prompted me to collect some of the experiences I lived through. Experiences that would give insight into the nature of fascism and communism, the hardships of arriving in a country without a penny and not knowing the language of the land. Experiences that reveal the immense difference between life in peacetime in a powerful, rich country and life under dictatorship, during war and revolution, in a poor land torn by the unfortunate circumstances created by history.

I escaped from communist Hungary through the Iron Curtain one month after the outbreak of the Hungarian Revolution, in the fall of 1956, after the Soviet army brutally crushed the uprising against communist rule. Although I moved thousands of miles away to the New World, I kept in close contact with my family in Budapest and followed the political and economic developments of Hungary and the region. My children were brought up as Americans but visited Hungary a number of times. They have been very interested in Hungary's recent history as they have seen it through their own eyes and through my past experiences.

Sometimes I envy my children for having grown up under relatively affluent circumstances. Television, telephones, overseas trips, driving a car at sixteen, central heating and air conditioning, CD players, and many other conveniences all came to them without their having to make an effort.

During the twentieth century, society has undergone a tremendous change. Even parents who grew up in the same country as their children often feel the generation gap is so great that their young ones are unable to understand and appreciate the life and hardships they experienced. The gap in my case, and in the case of many others who lived through political turmoil, is even greater.

It seems on the surface that my children's lives are much richer than mine was in my youth, but sometimes I wonder. When I tell Nicholas and Gordon about traveling on the tops of railway cars in search of food, escaping through the Iron Curtain, being shot at by a Russian tank, living in a bunker through the siege of Budapest, and surviving in fascist and communist regimes, I see in their eyes that perhaps they also missed something from life. Experiences that are unpleasant and frightening can also be unique, challenging, and character-molding. For the romantic, these adventures compensate for the lack of an easy road in life.

Despite the hardships I lived through, I, too, was lucky. I was lucky to survive fascism without personal harm, and I have been fortunate to experience the disintegration of communism that drove me and so many others from our homes.

Unfortunately, the defeat of Nazi Germany five decades ago and the Soviet Union's recent collapse did not eliminate the danger of fascism and communism in Europe. It has again become imperative that we remind ourselves what *dictatorship* means.

The purposes of fascism and communism are quite similar. Dictators of both ideologies use their fanatic beliefs to justify territorial gains for their respective countries and to eliminate other nations or their cultures in the process. In a complete turnabout, danger from the extreme right now comes from Russia. The Intercontinental Ballistic Missiles may not point at American cities any more, but the leader of a large political party in Russia is advocating fascist ideas: discrimination against a segment of the population and conquests of other nations' territories.

The recent resurgence of communism in Serbia caused the deaths of more than 200,000 people in the former Yugoslavia; the number of casualties there during these years of "peace" equals the number of casualties from the explosion of the nuclear bombs dropped on Hiroshima and Nagasaki at the end of World War II. Hunger, fear, rape, and mutilation of innocent women and children became everyday occurrences again, and refugees flooded into the Western and Central European countries. Ethnic cleansing, which reached its height during World War II, was openly advocated and practiced during the Bosnian war.

My wartime experiences occurred a long time ago. For millions in the Balkans, the wounds of war have not healed yet. But despite the intervening years, the practices of ethnic cleansing and extreme nationalism in these episodes in history are quite similar.

I have not attempted to write a historical study and cannot claim to be the central figure in any outstanding heroic act. My personal experiences are similar to those of many ordinary people caught up in a cruel sequence of events. I believe that no one can remain simply a bystander, escaping the effects of despotism, while living in a dictatorship.

THE BEGINNING
OF THE END

In the mid-1980s, forty years after the end of Nazi rule, I first realized that the fall of communism must be near, at least in my native Hungary. Visiting Budapest to attend a high school reunion, I found that, although the country was still under communist dictatorship, the expectation of freedom was apparent everywhere. Even the officials behaved differently, as I had the opportunity to experience upon my arrival. Instead of giving me a look "deserved" by a political dissident, the man checking my passport and visa at Budapest Airport was unusually polite, and at the green light section of customs the officer just waved me on with a smile.

"Do you think they will have free elections soon?" inquired my sons after I returned home.

The people's attitude in Hungary certainly indicated that the end of communist rule could not be far away. An incident representative of the changing times occurred on the day of my high school reunion.

On the Friday afternoon before our reunion dinner four of my former classmates and I visited our high school. The principal and his assistant were very friendly as they accompanied us through the familiar classrooms. We rewarded them with stories of events that took place during the war they were too young to have lived through or remembered. They laughed at our tales of mischievous behavior and practical jokes aimed at our classmates and sometimes our teachers.

Especially enjoyable were the colorful reminiscences of John Grétsy, a parson. As was customary in communist countries, John wore civilian clothes without his collar while visiting our former school. Priests in communist countries wore civilian clothes to protect not themselves but those with whom they associated. (John died years later after a long illness. His speeches from the pulpit must have also been successful. To express their appreciation, members of his flock from five villages came to his funeral in such numbers that a traffic jam ensued.)

Before we left, the principal asked what each of us did for a living. He nodded with satisfaction, hearing that Aladár was a doctor and chief of a hospital, Miki a well-known film cameraman, Otto a director of a factory, and I a city planner. I did not find it necessary to mention that I practiced my profession in the United States.

John was the last to announce his vocation, still in his jovial manner: "I am just a poor country parson," he said. We all laughed.

"Sure, sure," said the assistant principal, a woman, who was obviously the political appointee of the school. "Now tell us what you really do."

It took a little while to convince the principal and his assistant that John was indeed in the priesthood, but instead of the expected raised eyebrows or cool acceptance of this terrible fact, the assistant principal offered her right hand to John in a very friendly manner. "We can shake hands," she said, "after all, we're in the same business. I teach the theory of Marxism-Leninism."

We all laughed again, not because of the interesting comparison between religious and Marxist-Leninist beliefs but because of the fact that this subject could be discussed in such a lighthearted manner, among strangers, without fear of the secret police. During the Stalinist times we all would have been punished with at least a few years in jail for committing such a sacrilege against the prevailing communist "religion."

The next Sunday morning I enjoyed the beautiful panoramic view from the historic Castle Hill of Buda, overlooking the Danube, the Margaret Island, and Pest. Although not a churchgoing person, I slipped into the centuries-old Coronation Cathedral and stood behind the pews. At the end of Mass, the familiar words of the old hymn sounded, the nation's cry to its patron saint.

Please do not forget
Your poor Hungary,
Deliver its people
From this slavery.

I heard this hymn often in my youth, when it seemed the request might be fulfilled only in the distant future. On this occasion, instead of sadness and resignation, hope and anticipation of better times sounded through the voices and shone on the faces around me. I was not the only one whose eyes were moist.

Unfortunately, the road leading to this hopeful stage of history was long and tragic.

NEW YEAR'S EVE

The display of a wide variety of exotic drinks under palm trees was magnificent. Pretty waitresses rushed about, carrying trays with champagne-filled glasses. Across the bay, three large cruise ships, brightly lit with thousands of bulbs, docked at Nassau Harbor. Shining stars and perfect weather made this New Year's Eve memorable.

My wife and I toasted each other and moved toward the beach to watch the midnight fireworks. A spectacular colorful display it was, and the air reverberated with explosions.

Our sons mingled with the younger crowd at the popular resort hotel. For them, the sights and sounds of the fireworks represented just that—fireworks. Not for me. Memories of a New Year's Eve, also with loud and colorful explosions, but quite different ones, clouded an otherwise perfect evening.

Nicholas and Gordon often asked me about the siege of Budapest during the winter of 1944–45. I could not help comparing this New Year's Eve in the Bahamas to the one I spent as a child in an air raid shelter. A great contrast. In the Bahamas: an abundance of food and drinks, palm trees, beautiful weather, luxurious accommodations. During the other New Year's Eve, decades ago, when I was a teenager: the sounds of explosions coupled with death, destruction, cold, and hunger.

Just before Christmas of 1944, the Soviet army surrounded the entire city of Budapest. Inside the circle, the defending Nazi army; outside, the attacking Russians. The fragmented remains of a small Hungarian army were split between the two main warring forces, reluctantly following the orders of their respective allies, neither of which represented the country's interests. My fellow Hungarians, like many other nations in Eastern and Central Europe, knew they could expect no satisfactory conclusion to the war.

Unlike in Western Europe, the choice was not between a democratic or a totalitarian government. The victor would be either a fascist or a communist army. For a segment of society, mainly those with Jewish background, the Nazis with their mission of racial supremacy represented a graver and more imminent threat; others feared the communists more. Owners of businesses and large tracts of land knew they would be among the first to suffer from Marxist ideology. The communists would label all well-to-do persons as class aliens, punishing them with loss of property, freedom, at times even life. This unfortunate situation that was typical of the entire eastern part of Europe was well described by Gustav Herling in his book, *A World Apart.*

Herling was a Polish army officer at the beginning of the war. After the fall of Poland, a Soviet court sentenced him, based on trumped-up charges, to ten years of hard labor in a Siberian gulag. That conviction was equal to a death sentence, since the communists, like the Nazis, fed the workers in their camps an insufficient diet. When a prisoner became too weak to fulfill his work quota—cutting down trees in the Siberian winter or shoveling dirt in the summer—he received his death sentence. His meager food allowance was further reduced to a level inadequate for survival.

Herling was saved from certain death by Hitler's attack on Russia. An alliance was formed between Britain, the exiled Polish government, and the Soviet Union, and Herling was released from the gulag just when he was at the end of his endurance. He was allowed to rejoin the free Polish army, but memories of his terrible experiences in the gulag stayed with him.

"I think with horror and shame of a Europe divided into two parts by the line of the Bug," Herling wrote, "on one side of which millions of Soviet slaves prayed for liberation by the armies of Hitler, and on the other millions of victims of German concentration camps awaited deliverance by the Red Army as their last hope."

Our family had reason to fear both the Nazis and the Soviets. We were afraid that if the war lasted much longer the fascists would discover my father's involvement in saving Jewish lives and property; and we dreaded the Soviets, whose cruelty, especially toward class aliens, was well known.

We knew that Hungary's fate was sealed in 1941, when Pál Teleki, the prime minister, committed suicide under German pressure. He realized there was no way to keep the country out of harm's way. But though forced into the German camp, Hungary—unlike neighboring Slovakia, Romania, Serbia, and Croatia, which turned to fascism—was able to keep the small fascist party out of power until 1944. As a result, unlike in the rest of German-occupied Europe, refugees fleeing from Nazi rule in the late thirties and early forties found relative safety in Hungary until the spring of 1944.

Many of the thousands of political refugees were Jews, who easily obtained asylum in Hungary at a time when the Western countries were reluctant to grant visas to them. In Western Europe, outside of Germany, the inhuman treatment of Jews began after the armistice between Germany and France, when the elected French parliament named Marshall Pétain to head the collaborating Vichy government. Deportations there began in 1941; wearing the yellow star was introduced in early 1942. At that time, of the countries under Nazi influence or control, only Finland, Italy, and Hungary managed to refuse cooperation with the Nazis regarding the treatment of Jews.

A few days after March 15, 1944, when Hungarians still dared to celebrate a national holiday of independence from Austrian control, Hitler ordered the country's total occupation and the government's replacement.

"Looks like the Germans had enough of the Kállay Double," people remarked bitterly, in reference to the Hungarian folk dance, the Kállay Double, and to the Hungarian prime minister at the time of the German invasion, Nicholas Kállay. Many jokes were born, referring to Kállay's double dealings, his tough job of satisfying and at the same time resisting the powerful Nazis.

After the occupation the prime minister tried to avoid his fate and found temporary refuge at the Turkish embassy (the Turks were still neutral at that time), but the Nazis eventually deported him to Mauthousen and later to Dachau. Naturally, the Germans did not reveal Kállay's whereabouts.

The Hungarian colors we usually wore on the Ides of March reappeared on our lapels in protest of the Nazi occupation, but the German war machine was too strong for us to resist successfully.

Nazi rule affected the entire country, but people of Jewish origin suffered the most. Wearing the yellow star became compulsory for Jews in April, 1944, and deportations to Germany began soon after that.

By the time the fall of 1944 arrived, the situation in Budapest became critical for everyone. Nazi occupation and an internal fascist rule along with the threat from the Russian army placed us in a precarious position. Nevertheless, for the Christmas holiday season my family was together in Budapest, ready to celebrate. My parents, sister, and I stayed in my widowed maternal grandmother's apartment. We were waiting with concern and fright to see how the change of domination from one totalitarian country to another and the siege of Budapest would affect us. At the age of fourteen I was old enough to realize that great danger was facing our city and its inhabitants.

I was wondering whether luck or misfortune brought the family into Budapest for these trying times. We were not from the city originally. During the first thirteen years of my life our family lived in the village of Ujszász, on the Great Hungarian Plain. My father started working in Ujszász as a young man, immediately after finishing college, and lived there with his parents and sisters. At first he was an assistant in the municipal offices, and he later became a village manager. He met my mother and her family in the neighboring village, where my mother's father was also a village manager. Both families lived in Transylvania (now western Romania) while it was part of Hungary, until the end of World War I. Having a lot in common, members of the two families soon became friends.

My father started courting my mother soon after they met. The marriage ceremony was held in the Catholic church in Ujszász. Having been brought up in the Presbyterian faith, my father had to give dispensation according to the rules of the Catholic Church of those days. Dispensation meant that my father agreed to have his children be brought up as Catholics. He made this concession grudgingly. In his family he followed his father's religion and his sisters became Catholics after their mother's faith. Despite the dispensation, my father hoped that his son or sons could be brought up as Presbyterians. There was no problem when my sister was born, but after my birth, my aunts had to smuggle me out of the house to be christened in the Catholic church. My father was heartbroken but finally resigned to the facts. Fortunately, as a newborn, I was completely unaware of all the commotion.

For their wedding, my father intended to wear his World War I lieutenant's uniform in church. Wearing uniforms on special occasions was then a customary as well as economical practice. There was a small problem, however. The uniform would not be complete without the sword, a symbolic weapon, that still bore the initials of K & K, representing "Kaiser und King," signs of the Hapsburg Monarchy. As a rule, no weapons were allowed in the church, especially any that reminded people of centuries of Austrian domination. My father solved the problem.

"Those initials do not represent Kaiser und King," he explained to the priest. "They are my bride's and my initials."

A lucky coincidence that their names were Kathleen and Kálmán. The priest had a good laugh about my father's explanation and allowed him to don his full military outfit.

Ujszász was a poor agricultural village. Although electricity became available when I was a toddler, only two roads were improved with macadam surface. There was no running water, no sewers. We had an open well at the bottom of the garden, providing water for washing. For drinking water we had to go to the artesian well, whose water was yellow because of its mineral content. Out-of-town visitors, fooled by the color of the water, were sometimes shocked at our dining table, believing that everyone, including the children, was served wine from a water jug. We missed modern conveniences, but, on the positive side, in a community of about six thousand people, one hardly ever saw a policeman. Crime was practically nonexistent. My sister and I had a happy childhood in Ujszász.

In 1943 I was thirteen when my father took a village manager position at a resort along the Danube, near Budapest. We spent summers there, in Leányfalu. Prior to our move my sister, Ildikó, three years my senior, and I traveled by train every day from Ujszász to a nearby city to our high school, called a "gymnasium." Gymnasiums were for college-bound students and included grades five through twelve. At that stage of the war there were no buses running that could take us to a high school from Leányfalu, and the village had no train service. When my father started his new job, the family moved to Grandmother's apartment in Budapest on a temporary basis so that Ildikó and I could attend school in the city. Later our stay in the capital became permanent.

My first encounter with a Russian soldier occurred well before the Soviet army reached our area, while we were vacationing in Leányfalu. It happened during the summer of 1944 when the village was even then a happy, peaceful place, at least during the day.

The river was the lifeline of the area. Ferries, paddleboats (not unlike the ones on the Mississippi), and smaller propeller boats connected the towns with one another and the capital. I started playing tennis there, but water sports provided our main entertainment. There were plenty of boys my age with whom to share the fun. During the day only the occasional presence of German soldiers stationed nearby reminded us of the war and Nazi occupation.

The evenings in Leányfalu were not always so peaceful. The Russians started bombing Budapest, about fifteen miles away, during the protective cover of night. We could hear the Soviet planes' attacks, sounds of antiaircraft fire alternating with exploding bombs. At times we could see a "Stalin candle," a large ball of burning magnesium thrown from a plane, floating above the target area and illuminating it for the bombers.

During an air raid, while we watched the lights of the attack and listened to its sounds, my father and mother worried for relatives and friends in the city. Ildikó and I, with our youthful optimism, felt safe and secure. We knew our village had no military target, not even a railway line. When suddenly bombs exploded all around us, we were shocked and frightened. Apparently a critically damaged plane released its bombs over the village before crashing, destroying a number of houses, and killing and wounding people and livestock.

The next morning, at the crack of dawn, German soldiers drove up and down the village and the countryside on their loud motorcycles, claiming that a parachutist had been spotted. Their search was unsuccessful.

People walked around the village to assess the damage the bombs caused the previous night. They began mourning those who so suddenly and unexpectedly had fallen victim to wanton destruction.

The following day, a slightly wounded, thoroughly exhausted and frightened Russian airman appeared at the outskirts of the village. There was no need to fear his only weapon, a revolver. However, angry cries followed the Russian as a few men escorted him to the porch of my playmate Karl's residence.

The prisoner's "captors" chose to bring him to Karl's home because with its front porch open to the main street the house provided an excellent stage. As the procession approached the house, Karl and I were just getting ready to join our friends for a swim in the Danube. Instead, we decided to satisfy our youthful curiosity; we watched with open mouths and listened as people cursed at the Russian, blaming him for all the destruction.

"That monster deserves a rope," somebody yelled. "Bombing a village with no military or strategic targets. Why do you offer him a chair?"

The Russian just sat on the porch, his eyes moving nervously around. Those were not the eyes of a monster but of a young man, almost a boy, fearing for his life.

One person in the village, a former prisoner of war from Russia who elected to stay in Hungary after World War I, tried to have a conversation with him, but the Russian just watched the increasing number of spectators, expecting the worst. Eventually, Karl's mother noticed that the Russian could hardly swallow, his mouth was so dry. She placed a glass of water on the table but counterbalanced her kindness with an angry outburst: "You don't deserve it, you killer of innocent people."

At first, the prisoner eyed the water suspiciously but then decided to trust his "hostess" and gulped down the contents of the glass. The Russian's roving eyes still showed fear, but there was also a ray of hope in his expression.

"Why are you giving him water?" questioned someone. "What he deserves is a good beating." The comment met with approval from the crowd, but a middle-aged woman was much kinder. She looked at the Russian but saw far behind him. "He is just my son's age. I wonder how Johnny would be treated if he became a prisoner?"

Another woman approached the villager who spoke Russian. "Ask him whether he is hungry."

The question, repeated in his language, startled the prisoner. He shook his head, but without conviction. In a little while Karl's mother appeared with a piece of watermelon. Amidst conflicting shouts of protests and encouragement, the Russian gulped down the fresh fruit before the spectators could come to a consensus as to whether he deserved to be fed. A little while later when a hearty meal appeared on the table, nobody protested, but one young man went too far by offering the Russian a cigarette.

"Why not a cigar and an easy chair?" complained somebody, rather loudly. But our Russian—he was "our Russian" by then—interpreted the protest as encouragement and took the cigarette gratefully. Some people were already making plans for the prisoner's staying in the village following the war. After all, people recalled, we had acquired a Russian during World War I also. These plans suddenly ended when the German soldiers arrived and took the prisoner with them, ending the discussion about the Russian's future.

I do not know what happened to the Soviet airman, but his chances for survival were not good. Even if he outlived the German prisoner-of-war camp, he was probably taken to a Siberian gulag after the war. Afraid of the "contamination" of Western influence, Stalin ordered the deportation of most Soviet citizens who ended up in Western Europe during the war, with the exception of the fighting forces.

The summer over, we moved back to Budapest for our second year in the city. Life was faster and noisier along a main thoroughfare in the central area of the capital than in the relative quiet we were used to in Ujszász and Leányfalu. Ildikó and I enjoyed the hustle and bustle of the city. We liked living in Grandmother's apartment, which had become too big for her after Grandfather died and her son, Uncle Julius, moved out. On the second floor, right above the stores, three big rooms faced the wide József Boulevard. Before the air raids became frequent, I loved to sit on the wide windowsill in good weather, the wings open, with a book in hand, now and then watching the streetcars that rolled by or the people who sat at the outdoor cafés and ran in and out of stores. The five-story structure was built around a courtyard with uncovered corridors on each floor. From these corridors opened the doors of apartments whose windows looked to the side and back streets. The windows of our kitchen and a small room also faced the interior courtyard.

During the school year, living in Grandmother's apartment with all its conveniences was a vast improvement over village life. Taking the streetcar to school and not having to walk long distances were luxuries we appreciated. In addition, before the military front came close to the city's borders, we could enjoy productions in the numerous movie houses and theaters.

All of this changed during the fall of 1944. With the Russians' advance, the dangers of war became a reality for us. On one occasion my mother, sister, and I went to see a movie in a nearby cinema. The sentimental, light comedy, *Muki,* gave no acknowledgment to the raging war. We felt safe because we knew there would be plenty of time to find a shelter between the sound of sirens and the arrival of Soviet airplanes flying in large formations. For the approach of high-flying reconnaissance planes, the city's life did not stop; those planes carried no bombs, posed no immediate threat. At least not until that day.

We left the movie house without suspecting any danger, but as we drew close to our block we heard a tremendous explosion from the direction of our building and felt the subsequent blast.

"Your grandmother!" cried out Mother. "She is at home!"

A wall crashed with a tremendous noise. Bricks, pieces of furniture, and remains of human bodies blocked our path on the sidewalk. On one of the upper floors a bed tilted back and forth until it fell to the floor below and broke into pieces. Twisted steel beams pointed toward the sky accusingly. There were no screams, no moans. The dead do not cry. Small fragments of the rubble continued rolling down. Windowpanes were crashing to the sidewalk all over. Standing near the curb of the wide sidewalk, we tried to avoid being cut by the flying broken pieces.

"The key, Mother, the key!" I yelled, recovering from the sudden shock. "Let me run home and see what happened to Grandmother."

Running around the rubble as the dust settled I noted with relief that the bomb had fallen on the building next door, leaving ours relatively intact. Rushing through the gate, I took the steps three at a time and burst into the apartment. Grandmother tried to hide how frightened she was, but her shaking hands revealed her true state of mind.

"We're all right. Mother and Ildikó are coming," I said. She needed the reassurance. "They'll be here in a minute."

Our building suffered no serious damage. The old, five-story, brick buildings were well constructed; their solid fireproof materials could withstand much. The bomb destroyed only a part of the top three floors of the adjacent structure, slightly cracking the fire wall protecting our apartment. Its staircase intact, the remaining portion of the building next door was used throughout the remainder of the war.

Since there had been no air raid warning prior to the bombing, windows of some apartments had been kept closed during the explosion. Most apartment dwellers, however, were, like us, careful enough to close only the outside wings of the windows. The inside panes were saved from the destruction.

From the day of that bombing we kept all window panes open in our apartment, except during brief "warming" periods. Mother became more and more protective of Ildikó and me, curtailing our excursions outside the building. As soon as the sirens sounded, she ordered everybody to the shelter in the basement of our building without delay.

The schools were still open, but air raids frequently interrupted our classes. Students and teachers became more interested in saving their lives than discussing Pythagoras or Cicero. As soon as the sirens gave warning about the approaching Russian planes, we hurried home if there was enough time or found refuge in a nearby shelter. Finally, around November, with the front line reaching the outskirts of Budapest, the schools closed.

My father, who usually came home for the weekends on one of the small passenger boats that served the communities along the Danube, was barely able to reach the city before Christmas. He could not return to work after the holidays; by then all lines of transportation were cut off by the fighting forces.

Life went on during this holiday season, under the most unusual circumstances. Even during the fiercest periods of armed conflict, people continued their regular routine as much as they could. They worked, laughed, loved, fought with each other, and tried to act as they would under normal circumstances.

Despite all the bombing and constant artillery fire exchanges, inhabitants of Budapest showed a stubborn determination to observe the holidays. Opposing armies were ready to destroy each other and the city, but people continued buying Christmas trees and presents. Between air raids the women tried to prepare at least one special meal with whatever groceries they had saved or could obtain with food coupons.

I do not remember the Christmas presents we exchanged, but I still can see the tree lit not with electric bulbs but with real candles, as was customary in those days. Unfortunately, the night was neither as silent nor as holy as our singing indicated. The noises of war often interrupted our celebration in the cold apartment. We made sure that all the windows were swung open to protect the panes from being broken by explosions.

After Christmas, having been forced to spend more and more time underground, we carried beds, food, and other necessary items to the basement shelter. By the time New Year's Eve arrived, each of the tenants had claimed a certain portion of the basement as home. Still, at quiet periods we went upstairs to use the bathrooms, cook, or just enjoy a little privacy from the crowded accommodations of the air raid shelter.

New Year's Eve was the last time we saw signs of normal life on the streets, if one could call it normal. In the besieged city, with fierce fighting on the outskirts, people celebrated. Around midnight we heard horns and laughter from the streets. Was it crazy, reckless behavior, or did their natural defense mechanisms keep people from submitting body and soul to the tragic events? Whatever the case, it now seems such an absurd scene: residents leaning out the open windows and waving to the celebrating passersby, ready to run to the shelter any moment, wondering when and where the next explosion would occur!

Soon after New Year's Day we moved into the shelter permanently; the bombing and shelling became too frequent to stay upstairs for long periods of time. By then everyone was accustomed to the frequent explosions and antiaircraft fire—with the exception of two people.

Aunt Lili, as we called one old woman of enormous proportions, was constantly frightened. After every explosion she cried out: "They are shooting at us! This is the end!"

Ildikó and I liked to tease her.

"No, Aunt Lili, that was only a military truck's exhaust pipe backfiring," said Ildikó. "They don't get decent fuel, that's why."

Just about when Aunt Lili almost believed us, a large explosion shook our building. Jumping up, she yelled, almost more triumphantly than fearfully, "Was this a truck too? Was it? You see, I told you, this is the end!"

"It must have been a tank making that big noise, Aunt Lili," I said. "They backfire much louder."

She looked at us with contempt. "You kids make a joke of the war."

The other person who could not adjust to the hardships and danger of war was Mr. Cullan, a middle-aged, well-to-do man. He was near the breaking point. His extremely pretty young wife tried to console him, but he just sat at the edge of his bed for hours, rolling and unrolling his leather belt. Occasionally, he talked about a mine he owned in the eastern part of the country, now in Russian hands. Whether his pretty wife was as sorry as he was over the loss of that mine I do not know. I do know that she kept her eyes on the other men in the shelter more than on her panic-stricken husband.

Grandmother and my parents, although obviously concerned about our uncertain future, behaved quite calmly. Losing everything because of war was not unknown to them. My maternal grandfather, who died in the 1930s, had been expelled from Transylvania after World War I. When the Hungarian administration was replaced by Romanian occupation, the new rulers put Grandfather and his family in a cattle wagon and shipped them to Budapest with many other refugees. In the process, my grandparents lost most of their possessions, including a house. Even more painful was the loss of their firstborn daughter, who caught the Spanish flu in the unheated cattle wagon. A large photograph of my aunt Duci was beside Grandmother's bed until the day she died at the age of 101.

Within a few days of moving into the basement the building's tenants got acquainted and formed little social groups to pass the time. The main topic of the adults' discussions was the uncertain future awaiting us.

There was no electricity, and candles and kerosene lamps could be used only sparingly, to keep the air clean. Fortunately, water still trickled through the pipes.

Everybody hoarded enough food to last a few weeks on a strict diet. One retired judge and his wife, however, believed that meals could always be ordered and delivered by their favorite restaurant in the next block. Now they had to live on a few crackers and leftover pieces of dry bread. To their credit, they endured the hardships without complaints.

In the middle of the haphazardly arranged "private" areas that the tenants created in the large shelter was a small section occupied by a family who did not live in our building. Members of that family did not communicate with anybody; only the superintendent knew them. When I asked my mother who these people were, she silenced me. "Don't ask. Nazi troops still may come around. Just hope everything will be all right."

Luckily, there were no SS troops in the area. The regular German

Wehrmacht soldiers who occasionally stayed at the shelter were not interested in civilian matters.

During the first days of January the front line moved to within a couple of miles east of us, at the outskirts of the most densely populated area. After the siege of the city ended, residents of that section, especially the women, told stories of horror.

The puppet fascist government the Germans placed in power made a last effort. Head of the small fascist party was Ferenc Szálasi, who in 1938 was jailed for unlawful political activities; jailing Szálasi was the Hungarians' answer to the Anschluss, Germany's annexation of Austria. Not accepting the fact that the war was practically over, the fascists ordered, through radio announcements and posters, every man between the ages of seventeen and fifty to register for military duty. After some deliberation, my father, who was forty-seven, decided that there was less danger in registering than in facing a military court under martial law. During a lull in the air raids, he walked to the nearby army post in his World War I lieutenant's uniform that still fit him. Day after day the assembled "soldiers" waited for the war to end. In the evenings they were allowed to go home, and they did, as long as the air raids permitted them to do so. One morning the fighting intensified around the military post to the extent that it was impossible to return there. My father's short military career of that war was over, at least for a while, but a few months later he had to pay dearly for those few days in uniform.

Two other boys about my age, George and Zsolt, lived in the shelter, and I spent most of my time with them during the siege of the city. Zsolt's classmate Laci Huszár, a Jewish boy, who also lived in the building before the siege, hid from the fascists somewhere in the city. He had with him Zsolt's identity papers to use in case of an emergency.

My two friends and I were able to use our boyish energy to find entertainment in those difficult days. While our parents, far more sensible than we, worried about the raging war, hunger, and the future in general, we were playing cards, chess, and hide-and-seek in the labyrinth of the basement's storage area. All those activities were fun, but we longed for a little more rigorous exercise.

"Let's play some Ping-Pong," suggested George, who was always ready for mischief.

Zsolt and I looked at each other. "Where do you suggest we do that?" I asked, but I already knew he meant my family's apartment. George and Zsolt's apartments were on the fourth floor, much closer to danger than our apartment on the second floor.

With some reluctance, I agreed to George's suggestion. We sneaked up to our apartment a number of times and played Ping-Pong on the dining room table while airplanes were machine-gunning the streets. We were confident that a Russian bomb would not penetrate to the second floor, even if it fell directly above us. The Russian bombs were rather small, as the one that had dropped on the building next door demonstrated. Fortunately, our mothers never found out about these dangerous excursions, and Grandmother was not there to complain. Grandmother was not well versed in the purpose of ball games. Seeing us play in better times, she used to scold me: "Why do you hit the ball so hard? Your friend cannot hit it back."

Our secret Ping-Pong games ended abruptly with a great explosion near the building. We hurried to the shelter, frightened out of our wits and with some remorse for our behavior.

"Where were you?" My mother demanded.

"Playing with George and Zsolt," I answered evasively. Another great explosion saved me from further explanation. I was lucky that I could hide the truth from Mother. She and others started to discuss how close that bomb fell to our building.

There were no babies or young children in the shelter, but an old woman was living her second childhood, unable to grasp what was going on. Once, while the terrible noises of war raged outside, she called Ildikó over to her bed, pressed a banknote into my sister's hand, and, being partially deaf, yelled, "Would you, my dear, run over to the store and get me a fresh roll, please? My daughter gives me stale bread. I don't know why she treats me like that."

"It's late; the stores are closed," said Ildikó after some thought. It would have been too great a task to explain the real situation.

On January 13, my fifteenth birthday, Mother surprised me with the best birthday present I ever had. She opened a can of pears she had saved for this occasion, and I had the luxury of filling my stomach with a delicacy!

The following day it was unusually quiet. Unexpectedly and without putting up resistance, the Nazi troops disappeared from the area. They withdrew to the other side of the Danube to hilly Buda and blew up the bridges connecting the city's two parts. With this sudden move our neighborhood was saved from hand-to-hand, house-to-house fighting. In their hasty retreat, the soldiers who occasionally stayed at our shelter left behind a few bags of dried shredded carrots, which later helped me to launch my first enterprise.

We knew the Soviet army would arrive soon to take control of the area. Trying to protect us from the front-line soldiers, my parents put a few valuables in one room of the apartment and locked the door. My mother wanted to dye my blond hair a darker shade, lest the Russians would take me for a German. With some difficulty I managed to talk her out of it. Father hid the canned food, saved for emergencies, under the beds in the shelter. But how naive we were! People continued wearing watches, wedding bands, and other jewelry. After all, we thought, no soldier would rob any of us like a common criminal in the presence of all those people in the shelter!

It took a while before the extent of atrocities committed by both sides of the warring nations became known. We didn't suspect the real horrors of concentration camps, but we knew that the Nazis treated innocent people whom they considered enemies inhumanely. The individual soldiers behaved correctly, although at times in an arrogant manner toward the general population. Their cruel actions were of an organized nature, directed from their superiors and rooted in contempt and hatred for "inferior races." I was wondering how bad the Russians would be. I was pretty sure they would not treat us with the same consideration we showed the Soviet prisoner I had met the previous summer.

Meeting the first occupying Russian soldiers on January 15, 1945, was a startling experience. Those men did not remind me of the frightened young airman; they were people hardened by many years of fighting, ready for cruel actions, with little feeling for humanity.

3

FROM THE FRYING PAN
INTO THE FIRE

"This is me, with the Russian officer." My son Nicholas proudly presented the picture from his summer vacation. At seventeen, he had spent a couple of weeks in a camp in Hungary. On an excursion with his friends, they met a group of Russian soldiers, stationed in the country under the Warsaw Pact—officially as allies, in reality as occupying forces, to make sure that there would be no repeat of the revolution of 1956.

Nicholas asked the privates to pose with him for a photograph, but when they learned his nationality, the soldiers withdrew from the camera with obvious concern, lest their superiors punish them for fraternizing with an American. The officer, not as narrow-minded as his subordinates, smiled and stood in front of the camera with Nicholas, even putting his arm around him. My teenage son's personal contact with the Russian soldiers was quite different from mine in 1945.

After the Nazi forces withdrew to the hills of Buda on January 14, quiet reigned in our neighborhood, although from the far distance the sounds of war could still be heard. George, Zsolt, and I sneaked up to our apartment and peaked out the open window. Not a soul in sight, not a sound made nearby. The upturned cobblestones and twisted streetcar rails did not hamper anyone's way. Large cavities of bombed buildings looked like accusing eyes waiting for more punishment or healing. The once beautiful eclectic facades along József Boulevard now lacked the signs of prosperity and the building boom of the early twentieth century.

To us the unusual quiet seemed almost worse than the constant, steady noises of war of the past few months. It was eerie to see the dead city waiting for its fate. I often thought of this scene in relation to the famous

Gary Cooper western. Spying the enemy, Cooper says something like: "It's quiet. It's too quiet."

It *was* too quiet, even in the shelter. The adults decided that the apartment building's heavy wooden door should not be locked. The Soviet soldiers could break the door down anyway if they wanted to enter the building. Why anger them? All superfluous activities stopped, and we waited with concern for the Russians' arrival. That expected event dominated the not very lively conversation. Only Mr. Cullan stuck to his routine. He continued rolling and unrolling his leather belt, though with greater speed and determination. Even we youngsters were strangely quieter than at other times, almost subdued.

I made a halfhearted attempt to liven up the conversation. "Aunt Lili, they're not shooting at us any more."

The old woman stuck to her guns. "They will yet. They will, you'll see. That will be the end for us."

Mother interrupted. "Leave Aunt Lili alone. Eat something; who knows what tomorrow brings?"

I did not have to be told twice. In those days eating was on my mind all the time. Besides, under the circumstances, even teasing Aunt Lili did not seem much fun.

That day and the next morning, we waited. Then suddenly, around noon on January 15, we heard the sound of heavy boots on the sidewalk outside our building. The old woman living her second childhood and Mr. Cullan did not react to the noise the army boots made, but everyone else jumped up. We had mixed feelings of fright and relief; we were afraid of the Russians but in a way glad that finally the waiting and uncertainty would be over.

After a short period of quiet, the army boots approached the entrance to the shelter. A strong kick and a push opened the unlocked door, and a couple of soldiers jumped inside, with their submachine guns pointed at us. A few more Russians followed, searching the shelter with their eyes.

"Nemetzky? Nemetzky?" they asked, meaning "Germans? Germans?" We shook our heads, but the Russians kept their threatening stance. When they were sure that no German soldiers were hiding in the shelter to ambush them, the soldiers turned their attention to other things.

"Watch, watch, watch," said the leader of the first group of Russians as he stepped into the shelter, while another one concentrated on the women. We all stood, mesmerized, watching the soldiers as they nonchalantly waved their guns and collected our valuables. Watches, especially the smaller ones, were a novelty in the Soviet Union and were a sign of prosperity.

The people of Budapest have always been well known for quickly creating jokes for any occasion. Finding out the Russians' real poverty and thus their attraction to anything technical, especially small watches, this story was born right after the Soviet forces' arrival: A Russian soldier acquires an alarm clock, but it does not work, and, anyway, he finds it too big for his wrist. He asks a watchmaker to make two small watches out of the alarm clock. The craftsman, bewildered, opens the back of the alarm clock, and finds a dead fly in the mechanism. "Oh, machinist kaput," says the Russian with sorrow.

But it was not the time for jokes yet. During the previous months we had seen from the Nazis' behavior toward Jews that this war was different from prior ones. It was common knowledge through Nazi propaganda that the Russian soldiers were not exactly gentlemen. Still, it was hard to believe that warring forces could have such total disregard for humanity. My own thinking was influenced by books about World War I. Then, at least according to the books, gallant opposing forces respected each other and the civilians, even mourned the death of famous enemy "comrades." No, we could not think it possible that in the twentieth century fighting forces would be allowed, for a period of time, to loot, destroy, and rape as they pleased in the conquered territories.

The leader of the Russians was a captain, still standing at the door overseeing the activities. He looked and acted like a gang leader, not an officer. He did not partake in the looting himself but took possession of the valuables his subordinates collected.

After the soldiers liberated us from our valuables and carefully guarded canned food, they started eyeing the women. A husky fellow approached my mother and Ildikó, who was seventeen. He glanced back at the captain, who gave an approving nod. The soldier took another step toward Ildikó and stroked her face with mocking gentleness. "Babushka, Babushka," he said grinning.

Ildikó turned white as she realized the soldier's intentions. My mother was trembling with fear, and Father had the appearance of a desperate man. I knew that it would be impossible to resist the well-armed Russians. The severity of the circumstances finally hit me. Until that moment, the tragedies of war were events that happened to others, not to me and my family or friends. Yes, people died, were wounded, lost their homes in air raids, were taken to concentration camps, but those kinds of tragedies could not happen to me! At least I did not think they could, until I looked into the muzzles of those submachine guns and saw the determination in the eyes of the soldier approaching my sister, while the others grinned lustfully. There was no more youthful optimism, no more seeing things on the lighter side, no more letting the adults worry about the problems. I think it was then that I grew up and began to see the events as they were: real, tragic, and frightening.

At that crucial moment, when desperation reigned over us, a well-dressed woman who stayed at the back of the shelter suddenly demanded to see the Russian officer. Pushing past the surprised soldiers, the woman offered herself to the captain in return for protecting the other females. By this act she spared my sister and the other women from being raped and avoided a possible clash with the soldiers.

What at first seemed like a heroic sacrifice lost a little of its value when we learned that the woman was a professional call girl who later received certain benefits for her services. Nevertheless, her quick action saved many from the soldiers, and we remained grateful to her. The Russian captain made our shelter his second home and spent a lot of time there. He did not seem at all concerned about the lack of privacy and did not try to hide his amorous activities with the call girl in the large common room.

After that frightening incident with the Russians, we were less worried about material things. Our concern was to survive the war in good health and without the loss of personal freedom. There was good reason to be concerned. The Soviet Union needed slave labor, and its army was ordered to provide a certain number of prisoners. Every time Russian officers called all able-bodied people out of the shelter we obeyed with fear.

"Little robot, little robot" were the dreaded words. Hearing those orders we wondered whether the Russians indeed needed only a little work like dismantling barricades, or if they would order us on a march to Siberia.

"Let's always take our warm coat and boots to work," warned my father. "Who knows where we will end up."

"And some food," added Mother, "I don't think the Russians would feed you until you reached a camp."

What a relief it was every time the "little robot" turned out to be just that, a little work in the neighborhood. A friend of mine, Paul, about sixteen at that time, was not that lucky. He was rounded up to be transported to Russia. Outside the city limits his father caught up with the marching troops and offered himself in return for the release of his son. The Soviet soldiers did not care who filled in the quota; the guard shrugged his shoulders and allowed the exchange. My friend's father never returned.

The Russians picked up my unsuspecting uncle Julius, too, for a "little robot." He had to suffer through three years of imprisonment in the Crimea. As a doctor, he received slightly better treatment than other prisoners. Still, by the time he came home in 1948, Uncle Julius was in terrible physical condition. At times, cruelty toward the prisoners in the Crimea was similar to that in German concentration camps except that in the Crimea there were no systematic mass murders. The men were often beaten by the guards, who did not treat the workers as human beings. Sick persons who could not control their bodily functions at roll calls were forced to eat their own feces or vomit.

Uncle Julius was lucky. Occasionally he had a chance to have a decent meal. The Russians called upon his expertise when important communists were sick. On those occasions he received small but lifesaving rewards.

Breaking into the apartments in our city, the soldiers took anything they desired. Since Budapest was the first major Western city they saw, the Russians were overwhelmed with what to them seemed richness beyond belief: bathrooms in the apartments, and valuables, such as cameras, bicycles, watches, and jewelry, that were unattainable in the "workers' paradise." At first they angrily called us "bourgeois." That was a great insult in communist terminology, implying membership in the hated capitalist ruling class. It took a while for them to realize that the conveniences our apartments had were the rule rather than the exception in Budapest. The inhabitants of an entire city could not be bourgeois.

We were disappointed by the disappearance of valuables from our apartment, but the activities also provided a few humorous moments. My father was color blind, a fact he had not completely accepted. Once he decided to have a suit made without consulting my mother or anyone else and arrived at home with a bright red outfit. Although useless, the suit still hung in his closet, and a Russian soldier found it attractive. He took one of our bicycles and proudly rode around in circles in the inner courtyard of the apartment building. With the red suit, an army cap, a camera hanging from his shoulder, and a full complement of watches on his left arm over the sleeve of the jacket, he looked exactly like a monkey performing in a circus ring.

The small, encircled defending German force in Buda was reduced to trying to delay the Russians' advance. There, as elsewhere in Europe still under the German Army's control, the Nazis' days were numbered but their stubborn, useless resistance caused more casualties. We listened to the explosions coming from the direction of the Danube with concern, but the fighting in Buda did not seriously affect us. Still, we spent most of our time in the shelter. Together we felt more protected from the soldiers, especially since the Russian captain was residing with us in the basement.

A few weeks after the liberation from the Nazi forces, our friend Laci Huszár appeared. Laci, a Jewish boy, was a few years younger than me. During the last few weeks of 1944, Laci was in a "safe house" for children. The Swedish government, through their diplomat Raoul Wallenberg, and the Spanish Embassy had provided Swedish and Spanish documents and accommodations for thousands of Jews; daring Hungarians in the puppet government covered up by accepting the people in question as legitimate foreign nationals. The father of the first freely elected Hungarian prime minister after the 1990 election, József Antall, was one of those who was instrumental in helping to save many lives this way.

It is remarkable that at the end of 1944, in a country that was occupied by the Nazis, Jews still could be protected in an open, organized manner. The situation was totally different in the countries surrounding Hungary. Jews from Czechoslovakia started finding refuge in Hungary after President Edvard Beneš in Prague transferred his powers to Emil Hácha, a friend of Nazi Germany, in October, 1938. In Romania, deportation and systematic killing of Jews started in 1941, at the time of the attack on the Soviet Union. In November of the same year, the Slovak government actually requested the Germans to remove Jews from their country and agreed to pay five hundred Reichmarks for each person deported. When the Slovak parliament voted on the deportation of Jews to Germany, the only opposition came from the Hungarian representative, János Esterházy, who declared: "It is shameful that a government, whose president and prime minister claim to be good Catholics, deports its Jewish citizens to Hitler's concentration camps." Esterházy's defense of minorities' rights was interpreted as anti-Slovak not only during but after the war. He died in jail in communist Czechoslovakia.

In Serbia, the fascist government of General Milan Nedić, who was an officer in prewar Yugoslavia, started to participate in the ethnic cleansing of Jews and other nationalities in 1941. At the same time, the Nazis forced the cruel fascist Ustasha organization onto the Croats.

Unfortunately, by the second half of 1944, even in Hungary, the SS and their local fascist puppets managed to deport the majority of the country's Jews from the small towns and villages, where hiding and protecting people was far more difficult than in a large city. For those who perished there was little consolation in the fact that Hungary, the first in the region to give full citizenship to Jews, was also the last to buckle under the overwhelming Nazi pressure concerning their fate. However, in July, 1944, even the German-controlled Hungarian government refused to continue the deportations. In Hungary, a Jewish community more than 265,000-strong survived, by far the largest in the Central European countries that were under Nazi control during the war.

Shortly before the liberation of Budapest by the Russians in October, 1944, Szálasi's small fascist party took control of the government with the German's help. Szálasi's thugs, frustrated by the sabotage of their ethnic cleansing efforts, were planning to raid Jewish homes and the safe houses.

Laci decided to walk to the place where a friend, a twenty-two-year-old mother of a small child, was hiding at the home of gentile friends. Having in his possession Zsolt's documents, he felt relatively safe on the streets. "I believed," he later told me, "I was going to be all right with Zsolt's identification papers, unless the Nazis asked me to pull down my trousers." (In most of Europe circumcision was not performed on non-Jewish boys.)

Liberation found Laci staying at that friend's hiding place. Their joy over freedom soon turned into a nightmare.

Laci and his friend greeted the liberating Soviets with jubilation. They shook the hands of the seven soldiers who appeared at their doorstep and hugged them. The Russians were not satisfied with such an innocent outburst of love; they threw Laci's friend on the bed and forced themselves upon her. All seven of them. Meanwhile Laci and the child were forced to stay in the same room lest they call for help. Laci, a child of only twelve himself, took the little boy to a corner of the room and covered him so that he would not witness the ordeal.

Laci's mother was luckier; she survived the last few weeks of Nazi rule at the home of gentile friends and came to no harm.

Laci's father, a doctor, was taken by the Nazis to a concentration camp during the fall. Arriving home, or rather joining us in the shelter, Laci and his mother expressed great concern about what might have been the fate of Dr. Huszár. A few days later he appeared and happily reunited with his family. The surprise came when he met my father.

"Oh, Mr. Téglás, what a pleasure meeting you," Dr. Huszár burst out. "Thank you, thank you for saving my life."

My father was startled. "I do not know you, Dr. Huszár. Are you sure you've got the right person?"

"But of course! Although I am not surprised that you don't recognize me. I looked quite different when you last saw me."

The story slowly unfolded. Near the small municipality of Leányfalu, where my father was the village manager, the Germans had a camp where Jews were awaiting transportation to the Third Reich. At that time the fate of those who were actually transported to Germany and the facts about the death camps were not yet known. It was obvious, however, that those forced to Germany would be in great danger.

Occasionally, the commandant of the camp summoned my father and presented various demands such as living accommodations for the officers or hay for the horses. These demands had to be met, but my father always made an effort to extract something out of the commandant to relieve the prisoners' suffering.

On one occasion, when my father had to appear to receive a list of demands from the commandant, he noticed that a prisoner was lying outside on the ground in apparent agony. Before they conducted their business, my father asked the commandant what the sick man's problem was. The commandant just shrugged. "Who cares? He is just a Jew," he said, and presented his list of demands.

My father looked the commandant in the eye. "I will attend to your requests as soon as the ambulance picks up that man."

At first the commandant looked angry; then he shrugged again. "Please yourself."

Dr. Huszár—he was the sick man—recovered from his bleeding ulcer in a hospital in Budapest, and his fellow doctors were able to hide his identity from the retreating Nazis.

We might have never learned the extent of my father's activities protecting victims from the fascists but for this unusual coincidence. I did know that the contents of a locked room in Leányfalu in our house were the property of a Jewish couple. This fact alone could have gotten our entire family deported. Had the war lasted much longer, there is no doubt in my mind that we would not have been able to keep my father's activities a secret.

Once during the summer of 1944, my father almost got into trouble for a far less serious action than protecting Jews or Jewish property. People of German origin living in Hungary and in other countries outside of Germany were encouraged by the Third Reich to join a special fighting military unit, the Waffen SS. Responding to the appeal, a young man of seventeen presented himself at the village hall to request identity papers. My father tried to talk the young man out of his move. When that failed, he simply delayed issuing the documents. A couple of weeks later the irate parents threatened to report him for anti-German activities. My father had to comply with their request. The young man went to protect his Fatherland and never returned.

Only after the war when a few people visited us to express their thanks did we learn about most of my father's deeds; he never spoke about them. When questioned, his usual comment was "I only did my duty as a human being."

Unfortunately, my father's attitude of honor did not belong to the world that we lived in after the war. His profession in municipal management was among those singled out by the communists because of its influence in village politics. Village managers became the victims of the "class struggle." My father could have obtained an advantageous position had he referred to his activities during the war. Mother begged him to do so, but, stubborn man that he was, my father flatly refused. His answer was always the same: "I only did my duty as a human being." He could not survive in a society where people lost their livelihoods only because they were "class aliens."

Laci was a good companion for us, and now the four of us boys tried to take advantage of the free time we had. Once we had a scare when the Russian captain wanted to play chess. I had the dubious honor of facing him as he sat there with great self-confidence. After all, the Russians are the world's best in chess. I was a pretty good player myself. In later years I represented my school in the interscholastic chess team with my friend Toni.

I was wondering. "Should I beat him if I can, or just throw the game?" I knew that the Russian had seen us play before and was afraid he might be suspicious if I made obviously bad moves. Perhaps I was overly concerned, but in those days one could never know. I sensed that wounding the conqueror's pride could be dangerous and might result in repercussions. More so, I feared, if the captain had a few drinks before our game. During his frequent drinking bouts he behaved in an irrational manner, threatening with his loaded revolver all those who were in his way. To relieve the tensions of war, many Russian soldiers drank until they were out of control. Some of them would drink anything they could lay their hands on. Expensive cognac or cheap mouthwash had the same value for the hardiest drinkers.

My father came to our table and warned my friends, reminding them of the golden rule: *kibitz,* be quiet. I motioned to Father to move away. If there was going to be trouble, I knew it would be better if there were no adults around.

I offered the captain the white pieces, but he rejected the advantage and placed a black pawn in one hand and a white pawn in the other, hiding from me which hand held which piece. That was a promising start. "Maybe he is a good sport," I thought. The captain started with white anyway, since I picked the hand with the black piece. He opened with the king's pawn, and I responded with my favorite move, leading to the French Defense.

Father watched with concern from a distance, while Mother engaged the call girl in a conversation. I soon became immersed in the game and forgot about the unpleasant circumstances. My friends kept quiet as we approached the end-game, with the captain having only his king and a pawn against my lone king left on the board. White could not place his king in front of his pawn in time, and in that position it is not possible to convert the pawn for a queen against proper defense.

What an ideal position! The Russian had a little advantage to boost his ego; on the other hand I could play for a stalemate. But should I? Would it be wiser to make a mistake at this position? I decided that making an error would be too obvious. After playing a good game I could not make a silly mistake without arousing suspicion. I pushed my king into the proper square, establishing the stalemate.

My nerve-racking chess game ended, and the officer was gracious enough to accept the draw, without asking for a rematch, to our great relief.

Gradually the tenants prepared to leave the shelter, carrying belongings up the stairs. It was not yet safe to stay in the apartments for long periods of time. The roving Russian soldiers still represented a danger, especially for the women. Besides, in the middle of winter it was too cold in the apartments.

"I don't know how we could move upstairs," complained my mother. "Even if it were safe, we would be freezing."

"Don't worry about the cold, Mother," I replied, "I'll take care of that problem."

The four of us boys sneaked up to the large attic of the building and collected fragments of the huge beams torn by small artillery fire to use in the stoves. When there were no more easily collectible pieces of wood, we did not shy away from cutting a few supporting beams as well. It was amazing how much unnecessary extra material was in those old structures.

We were lucky that our building sustained only minor damage. Some of the other areas of Budapest were destroyed; entire city blocks were in ruins. Concern for survival somewhat overshadowed our feelings for our beautiful city's demise; still, we learned with horror the extent of devastation. The view along the Danube was the most tragic. The beautiful luxury hotels on the Pest side were destroyed, and the magnificent buildings of Castle Hill in Buda seemed to be in a condition beyond repair. Spans of bridges connecting two sides of Budapest lay useless in the Danube.

The remaining German forces in Buda surrendered, and the Russian military patrols started policing the city, ending the period of free looting and rape. From that time on the heavy wooden door of the apartment building was kept locked day and night. Finally, we felt relatively safe from the Russian soldiers and were able to move upstairs permanently. Actually, most of the Russian soldiers were not bad souls, but that was no consolation for those who met the others.

With the war still going on, there were not enough military police. Occasionally, when drunken soldiers tried to break down the doors of the apartment buildings, usually during the nights, we used an improvised telegraph system. We leaned out the windows and yelled as loud as our vocal chords would allow, calling for the Russian military police.

"Patrule, patrule!" we yelled, and followed with the address of the threatened locality.

Soon, the entire city would be awakened by the cries, and everyone would repeat the message. Jungle telegraph, reinvented. If the Russian patrol did not show and the soldiers seriously threatened to break down the door, as a last resort we threw bricks and other heavy objects from the windows, careful only to frighten, not hurt, the attackers.

After the soldiers retreated from one apartment building, the whole thing usually started all over again a few streets away. "Patrule, patrule!" At times we found the entire scene somewhat amusing.

One day, I was looking out the window when a Soviet military police vehicle stopped in front of our building and three soldiers requested entry. I did not think much of it until the soldiers' heavy footsteps stopped in front of our apartment. The destination of the three Soviet soldiers was our home.

Mother responded to the loud knocking. Opening the door, she immediately realized that something terrible was happening.

Going through the captured military papers, the Soviet army found Father's name among those who were called up for service during the last few weeks of fighting in our area. Forcing their way into the apartment, the Russians grabbed Father and took him away. His requests to change his clothes and talk to us were rudely rejected. We did not even have the opportunity to say a proper good-bye.

I followed my father and the three soldiers down the staircase to the street. The Russians shoved Father into the car and quickly sped away. Looking up, I saw Mother in the window, leaning out to get a last glimpse of the disappearing vehicle. I slowly walked up the stairs. By the time I went into the apartment Mother had collapsed in a chair, crying. "We may never hear of him again," she said.

Father was taken prisoner to an unknown location, just when we believed that our family survived the war without personal harm. At that time I was only worried about my father and did not realize yet that to a large extent sustenance of our family had fallen upon my young shoulders. It seemed ironic that tragedy struck us after the siege of the city was well over, after we had survived much more difficult times, in the shelter. None of us would have thought then that about a decade later tenants of the apartment building would meet again in the shelter during the 1956 revolution, after fighting broke out between the Hungarian people and the communist rulers and occupying Soviet military forces.

4

BUSINESS FOR SURVIVAL

"Thank God for New York pizza," exclaimed Nicholas, arriving home for a break from his university.

As was his custom, Nicholas picked up a few slices of pizza from Broadway Pizzeria on his way to the house. Both my boys claim that nowhere is Italian food as good as in the New York area, not even in Italy.

His craving for good pizza launched Nicholas on his first business endeavor in Hungary, of all places, when that country was still controlled by the communists. At the age of seventeen, Nicholas spent a few weeks in a summer camp in southern Hungary, along the Danube. In addition to attracting youngsters from Hungary, the camp also provided a pleasant vacation for boys and girls of Hungarian descent who lived in North America or Western Europe. Every day, following a couple of hours of learning about his heritage, Nicholas enjoyed the companionship of his new friends and the fun of participating in water sports and other activities.

After about a week, despite having a great vacation, Nicholas had a feeling that something was missing: there was no pizza on the menu. Undaunted, he bought the necessary ingredients at the local store and prepared a pizza pie with the help of the women who did the cooking. Nicholas didn't get to eat much of the pie as the other Western boys and girls pounced on it before he could get a second slice. From then on, Nicholas made pizza every other day, selling the slices for a modest amount of money to cover his expenses, and had the satisfaction of launching a successful "business venture."

My first business effort also involved selling food, soon after the siege of Budapest, when people of the city were preoccupied with obtaining anything edible for their mere sustenance. I acquired one of the sacks of shredded, dried carrots that the hastily retreating Wehrmacht soldiers left in our shelter. For weeks we put off using the unappetizing contents of the sack. Even after our food supply began running very low, I craved for a greater diversity in my diet than cooked shredded carrots. I decided that the solution was to market my prized possession and supplement Mother's cooking with other edible goods purchased with the proceeds of the sale.

I realized that even in hard times such as the ones we lived in, packaging could improve marketing. A few stores had already reopened. I had the opportunity to buy cellophane and, with the help of my sister, created neat packages, each containing a good cupful of shredded carrots.

A small table and chair in front of our apartment building became my "store." A large sign advertised the "uniquely prepared and preserved vegetable delicacy." The speed with which I sold the entire contents of the large sack surprised even me. I was then able to obtain other, more appetizing foods, although with less appealing packaging than what my merchandise had.

Now that my father was confined in a Russian prisoner-of-war camp, our family had a tough time making ends meet. At fifteen, I was growing fast and had serious difficulties with my wardrobe. I remember wearing shoes whose soles had large missing areas. I did not worry much about minor problems like that. Besides, when I walked carefully without lifting my legs high, no one else could see the soles of my feet. Toni, my friend and classmate, was much taller than I and was able to use his father's clothes.

"I have to go home early again. My father needs our pants," Toni would say. "We have only one pair, the rest were liberated by the Russians." I never quite believed him; Toni loved to make mockery of the hard times. It took me a couple of years before I also grew into my father's clothes.

Although school had started, lectures were held in the yard until workmen could repair bomb damages. The routine of work and life in general slowly returned to the city, but it was far from normal. Food became available with ration cards but not in sufficient quantities. We were always short of cash. The fact that cigarettes were also available only on ration cards helped us. Nobody in our family smoked, but I bought the cigarettes with the ration cards and started a minor black market operation after school hours. The experience of selling cigarettes, using the money to buy more and selling them again at the busiest street corner of the city, taught me a lot not only about business but about underground sex life as well.

I remembered these events a few years ago, when Nicholas called me from San Francisco, where he worked a summer internship.

"It's terrible," he said. I could hear in his voice how upset he was. "It happened to me three times. Today a guy made a pass at me again."

I could not hide my amusement.

"There is nothing to laugh about. It's not funny," said Nicholas. "It's embarrassing. I don't know what to tell them."

"No reason to be upset," I said. "Take those approaches as compliments of people who live an alternative lifestyle. No harm will come to you; you don't have to participate." Still chuckling, I tried to picture my six-foot-two athletic son, embarrassed, as he rejected the unwanted advances.

In the postwar turmoil the police in Budapest had other things to do besides worry about sexual crimes, like the activities of pedophiles, who took advantage of the lapse of enforcement against their solicitations. Dressed neatly in shorts, fifteen, and blonde, I became a target. While I stood on the busy street corner offering my cigarettes for sale, certain customers tried to befriend me with unpleasant frequency. I did not realize their intentions until one of them offered me a movie ticket as partial payment for a purchase. Happy to avoid the long line in front of the theater, I accepted the barter deal.

We sat side by side in the movie house. Halfway through the main attraction the middle-aged man revealed that his interests lay in a subject other than what was on the screen. Placing his hand on my bare leg he whispered into my ear: "Aren't you cold in those shorts?"

Bewildered, I shook my head, but evidently with insufficient emphasis, because the man's hand started sliding higher up my leg.

I never learned whether the American warship sank the German U-boat or not. Leaving in a hurry from the middle of the row, I stepped on a few toes and elicited unpleasant remarks about my disturbing the show. I vowed at that moment to concentrate on my "business" and not befriend any of my buyers.

After a while, quite a few of my "colleagues" and I started selling and buying not only cigarettes but other items as well. Nobody could really say whether our wheeling and dealing was illegal; life had not returned to normal times when the legality of our business activities could be questioned. Survival was far more important than minor legal questions. A few months later things changed; the temporary authorities decided to eliminate the very active black-market operation that concentrated on selling items purchased on coupons at lower prices. Learning about the newly announced prohibition of selling on the streets, I hurried to unload my merchandise.

Little Joe, a fellow "businessman," was beside me when the policemen arrived to clear the street corner. If caught, no serious punishment would have awaited us, but we did not want to risk the possible confiscation of our merchandise. Little Joe jumped into a horse-drawn buggy whose driver was waiting for customers at the taxi stand. The horse and buggy business was revived for a short period of time after the war, until the taxi fleet was replenished.

"Come on, hop in," yelled Little Joe. I did not need further encouragement.

"All right, let's go out in style," I shouted back, and handed a banknote to the startled driver, who realized that we were indeed customers and not just some rowdy kids. Not sparing the horses, he quickly started driving. A few blocks away, we stopped the buggy, and I said good-bye to Little Joe and to our black-market operations.

I had to find another source of income, but what could that be? With the little time I had after school and homework, ordinary labor was out of the question. The opportunity arose when more stores started opening, some of them selling parts for all kinds of machinery. Most of the factories were still idle but trying to start production. With international trade nonexistent, there was great need for secondhand parts. It caught my attention that among the items in demand were ball bearings. This was valuable information, since I had an idea how to obtain those sought-after parts.

After researching the need, I took a trip to a makeshift junkyard, one of a number of such places on the outskirts of the city where wreckage of tanks and other military vehicles were piled up. Kids were playing war in realistic surroundings.

"Three-seventy-five!" yelled one of the boys, peeking out from under the wreckage of a Tiger tank. "You're dead!"

"Four-twenty-seven," sounded another cry from behind a Russian T34. "You've had it too!"

The boys were playing a game called "numbers war" that was popular among Hungarian youth. Members of two teams tied large cards with numbers on their heads, one number on the front and an identical one on the back. The cards of the two teams were of different colors. The object of the game was for one team to occupy the other team's territory and "kill" the enemy by reading their numbers, while keeping their own numbers out of sight.

When the battle was over, one of the boys turned to me. "You want to play?"

"Yes, but a different kind of game," I said, and explained my plan.

It did not take long to convince the warring team members that extracting ball bearings from the abandoned vehicles would be just as much fun as playing war games, and profitable besides. After arranging a truce and permanent peace between the two teams, I gave them information as to the marketability of the different sizes and makes of the ball bearings. "Look for the inscription. SKF brings extra money. Swedish make, the best."

Once more I had a flourishing business that stretched into the summer months. It was a far more satisfying activity than the black-market operation. The boys who extracted the ball bearings were happy with my payments, and I had the pleasant feeling of contributing something useful to the crawling economy. Unfortunately for me, the junkyards eventually fell under the supervision of authorities, and again I had to look for another way of supplementing the family's food supply.

My concern was urgent. At that time, one of the worst periods of inflation in modern history began. Currency in any denomination was practically worthless. During the time it took to receive payment and quickly spend the money, 90 percent of its value could be lost. Workers needed at least some of their compensation in food in addition to their pay. I remember seeing people in the parks not with dogs but with chickens on leashes.

I came to the conclusion that in the countryside the food shortage couldn't be that bad. On the other hand, because of the lack of organized channels of distribution, people in the small villages couldn't get simple items of clothing and materials such as threads and needles.

"You can't go alone," protested Mother. "It's still dangerous. The Russians may pick you up. And where would you stay?"

"How much food do we have left?" I asked. Mother did not answer. I knew I had made my point. "I'll be all right," I assured her. "There will be a lot of other people traveling."

I was right about that. I was not the only one who wanted to visit the countryside with my knapsack full of materials for trade. The great hunt for food was on. It was rather like a replay of the gold rush in the American West.

Trains began to run, slowly and not with great reliability, but they were running. The war decimated the rolling stock, especially the locomotives. A number of the 424 series steam locomotives, products of the Hungarian Ganz factory, survived. These great engines soon were supplemented with a large fleet of "Trumans," the nickname of locomotives designated with the series 411. They were manufactured for the invasion of France and unloaded by the Allies to various countries in Europe immediately after the war. One could recognize the distinctive "clickety-clickety" noise of the Trumans from a long distance. Thinking of my previous business venture I suspected that perhaps these locomotives might not have SKF ball bearings.

Travel to the country by train was definitely not first class. On the way to a remote village, I had to climb to the top of a car since the carriages inside were packed. The good-natured but very proper conductor joined those of us on top occasionally and demanded valid tickets, just as if we had been sitting comfortably in plush seats on an express train.

To protect our eyes from sparks, we had to turn our backs to the locomotive. Walking on the top of the car was dangerous when the train was in motion. At the stations there wasn't enough time to obtain entry to the toilets. We had to relieve ourselves behind trees and bushes, hurrying back to the train at the locomotive's whistle. The day went by without major discomfort, but the early fall night was cool, although I was wearing a pullover. The chilly air felt much colder on the fast-moving train, and I was shivering. I was able to doze off for only a few minutes at a time. Not exactly the sleeping accommodation my mother had in mind. The cold had one benefit: it kept me awake and safe from falling off the moving train.

I stayed on the train until the last stop, near the Romanian border, hoping that the farther I was from Budapest the better the deals I could make. In the small village where the train stopped, I headed first toward the clothing store. The sight of empty shelves gave me confidence for bartering. I offered my father's clothing—shirts, socks, a sweater—and other small useful items such as sewing materials to the farmers in exchange for such delicacies as smoked ham and white flour. I was careful to accept only those deals that I was sure made my trip worthwhile.

Besides obtaining food, my first trip had an interesting result. I had the opportunity to sleep with a woman. Literally—just sleep with her. A more accurate description is that I shared a bed with a woman, a fellow city dweller in search of food. We were bartering in the same farmer's house when we realized that it was too late to catch the last train back to Budapest. After spending one sleepless night on the top of a railway car, I longed for a decent rest.

The farmer was somewhat annoyed when I rejected his offer for the last two shirts I had. "All right, all right. So what else do you want for them?" he asked.

"Do you have a place where I could stay for the night?" I asked.

"I was going to ask you the same thing," said the woman.

The farmer thought about our request for a while. "I have only one bed available." He shrugged his shoulders. "It's big enough for two."

The woman turned to me. "How old are you?"

I blushed. "Fifteen."

"It's an emergency. We both need a good rest. You look like a decent fellow; we'll share. Head to foot." That meant our heads would be at opposite ends of the bed.

The farmer included in his deal a dinner and breakfast. Exhausted from the previous night's trip, I slept well, head to foot with the woman.

The trip was well worth it; we did not go hungry. At least, not very hungry. But telling my family about my sleeping accommodation was a mistake. Ildikó did not miss the opportunity to tease me. "Now I know why you are so anxious to travel to complement our diet!" she said.

Seeing and enjoying the results of my trip, Mother did not protest when I declared my intention of traveling to the countryside once more before it would become really cold. She even suggested where I should go.

"Your Téglás grandfather and grandmother were teachers and your grandfather the principal of the elementary school in Ecsed," she said. "Why don't you go there?"

Ecsed is in the eastern, least advanced part of the country. I had to make a number of train connections, waiting for hours at stations to reach the village. Arriving during the day I headed toward the school. When my grandfather moved there around 1905, the two-story building was a novelty. On the Hungarian plain, in general, there were no multistory structures. Grandfather's apartment was on the second floor of the building. My aunts told me that the first day they moved in the new building and leaned out the window a young boy who walked by looked up, amazed. "How did you get up there?" he asked. "On a ladder?"

I approached a woman on the street and asked a few questions about the school. She answered, but looked at me with curiosity. "Why are you interested in the school?" she asked. "You're too old for it. Anyway, where are you from?"

"I came from Budapest," I answered. "To exchange goods for food. I am interested in the school because my Téglás grandparents taught here. Did you know them?"

"Principal Téglás and his wife? Of course I knew them," she answered and then smiled. "The old man liked his wine. But he was a good man. He and his wife taught us much. Not just in the school and not just to read, write, and count. The principal taught my husband how to become a beekeeper. It served us well."

"That's good to hear," I said.

She changed the subject. "What have you got to sell?"

I pulled out a few items from my knapsack. She nodded in approval and motioned with her head. "Come this way. I'll give you a good deal."

On the way to her house the woman looked at me again. "Fancy seeing his grandson," she said to herself.

The major prize of my barter deal was a large rabbit. A female, pregnant rabbit at that. But the most memorable event of my trip was not my successful bartering. On the way back home, at a transfer station I was trying to find a place on the jam-packed train. Just when I was about to give up, I noticed that an enterprising passenger occupied one of the locomotive's bumpers. I quickly hopped up on the other guard, hugging my knapsack and a basket with the rabbit inside. My friends later listened with awe when I told them my experience of traveling on the bumper of a 424!

The bathroom and pantry windows in our apartment building opened onto light shafts. Light shafts are tiny courtyards, about the size of elevator shafts. They provide air and some light to the apartments' bathrooms, toilets, and pantries that have no windows toward the street or interior courtyard. Since our unit was on the second floor directly above stores, we could go through a door from the pantry to the ground floor of a shaft. My rabbit found a home there, and lived happily with her offspring. Considering the babies' fast growth and our desire to have meat on the table, the rabbit family's life span was rather short.

I was wondering how long we could go on without my father. We had not heard from him since he was taken prisoner. Our family wasn't the only one worrying about the whereabouts of loved-ones. Almost all who survived the war had somebody close to him or her who perished on the front, in Nazi concentration camps, or through other actions of the hostilities. The young male population was decimated. Many parents were mourning, or hoping for a letter from Russia, indicating that their son was alive. We were fortunate. One day a strange woman appeared at our door and asked for my mother.

"Mrs. Téglás, I have good news for you," she said. "Your husband is free. He is staying in our village and will be home soon."

At first Mother was suspicious. "Why is he sending a message instead of coming home?" she asked.

"He is ill. But here is a letter from him."

Father arrived home a couple of weeks later after the local doctor in the village had cured him of a serious stomach ailment. He told us the story of his relatively short imprisonment of less than a year. The first thing that happened to him soon after his arrest was a good beating he received for not reporting to the invading army that he was a former soldier.

"I am from the security forces," announced his interrogator. "Not everything you heard about us from German propaganda is true, but at least half of it is. So you'd better tell us what crimes you committed that you were afraid to report to our army. We have methods to squeeze the truth out of you."

When the Russians learned the circumstances of his enlistment, they stopped further corporal punishment and sent my father to a prisoner-of-war camp within the country, not far from Budapest.

He was one of the few lucky ones who were released before the Russians took them to Siberia or some other godforsaken place. He became seriously ill, unsuitable for transportation. Along with the sick ones who were released was one healthy prisoner who gained his freedom because he accidentally fell into the latrine and the unpleasant smell could not be scrubbed out of him. The next person who jumped into the latrine on purpose to try to avoid further imprisonment did not achieve his goal. The Russians realized what was going on.

Although not in his profession in municipal management, my father was able to get a job with a private company that was printing forms used in municipal offices. Life became easier. I was able to concentrate on my studies in tenth grade, although I still got involved in some business deals unique to those years. One of my ventures involved a couple of bicycle inner tubes. Since my bike had been taken by the Russian soldiers, I had no use for the tubes. Or at least I didn't until the season arrived to preserve bottled fruit. Ildikó and I cut the tubes into small rings and packaged them, creating a merchandise that was much sought after. The rubber rings were used to seal the cellophane on the glass jars. An item worth hardly anything under normal circumstances became of great value since it could ensure the safe preservation of precious food for the winter months.

For a couple of years we enjoyed significant economic improvement in Hungary. I concentrated on my studies full time, preparing for my tough high school final exams and entry to a university. I also had time to resume my favorite sport, tennis, and participated in tournaments, winning a number of trophies in my last year as a junior player. Unfortunately, the period of economic improvement and relative political freedom was cut short. What might have been the beginning of a free society turned out to be nothing more than a transition to communist rule, under pressure of the Russian occupying forces.

5

REINVENTING
THE WHEEL

"The university I choose should have nice tennis courts and a good football team," declared Nicholas as we were driving south on I-95 toward Washington.

I risked a mundane question. "Should it have a good business school as well?"

"Yes, yes, of course, but I would like to have a good time during my college years."

How could I argue with my son for wanting a good athletic program? After all, during my college years it was my participation in the tennis team that helped save my sanity. Without that outlet, life may have been unbearable during the Stalinist years.

As a senior in high school, Nicholas finally got down to serious thinking and research to choose a place of higher learning. Discarding his previous ideas of becoming an architect, a teacher, and a lawyer, he finally decided on business school. A business school that needed a place kicker for its football team.

I was happy about my sons' interest in sports and took some credit for their achievements since I taught them tennis and soccer. I began coaching their soccer team with the American Youth Soccer Organization when Nicholas was seven and Gordon six. Responding to a newspaper notice, I appeared with the boys at the organized meeting for the soccer group at the local recreation department. Realizing that I'd grown up in Europe, the other fathers immediately named me the soccer coach.

I had my reservations. "Yes, I played soccer as a kid, but I am a tennis player."

"You're the only one with an accent. We know nothing about kicking the ball."

That convinced me. At the time this conversation took place, soccer programs for young children had just started in our area. But what a start! It was fun watching my boys and their teammates in uniforms and proper soccer cleats as they reacted with great enthusiasm to the whistle of the official referee, on a full-size field. What a luxury for children so young. Some of them could not yet appreciate the game fully, I observed as I watched a player emerging from the mud he seemed to enjoy more than the game itself.

"Coach," he yelled, searching for me with his eyes, "which way are we going?"

On one occasion, when the game was not very exciting, I became immersed in my thoughts and neglected my duties as a coach. I was thinking of my recent trip to Hungary, when my sister Ildikó drove me to Ujszász, the village where we lived as small children. My mind wandered from the game at hand as I recalled the strange experience of arriving by car. In our childhood the customary transportation was the train. Not that automobiles were not available in those days: there were two of them in the village. The doctor and the vet had one each. Sometimes these old vehicles were actually able to perform their intended functions rather than serve only as symbols of wealth and social status. One of the first places Ildikó drove by was Mulberry Park, our favorite place for pickup soccer games.

I became a soccer coach in the United States because I have an accent. In our village Julius was destined to be the captain and center forward of our team, because he had THE BALL, the only official soccer ball our group of boys possessed. Of course we had no uniforms, referees, or coaches, and no enthusiastic parents to cheer during games and provide us with slices of fruit and other refreshments.

On the way home from school was our favorite time to stop for a quick game, despite the tiring trip following a long day. From fifth grade on, we had to travel to the city about twelve miles away, but not on comfortable school buses that pick the students up and drop them off near their homes. We got up at five in the morning and walked half a mile to the train station. After reaching the city of Szolnok, we had another mile-and-a-half walk from the station to our school. Making the trip twice a day was a lot of work, but we made the best of it. On the train, a coach was reserved for the students. This railroad car became our private club where we played games like hangman and battleship or just horsed around. The two daily train rides provided plenty of entertainment.

As we drove past Mulberry Park I realized that students in my boyhood village were now saved from the inconvenience of traveling to the city, but at a price. A new school building occupied the playground where we used to kick the ball, play marbles, and hunt the slow-flying june bugs. Near the school, a new house replaced our old residence. The fence was still there with the gate where the little gypsy girl used to request admission. She was about six years old and went from house to house to perform her "one-man show." I still remember the song Ildikó and I liked the most.

Steve is a charmer with dark brown eyes,
Likes to chase women like other guys,
I try to reach him but he shrugs me off,
I love him still and that is enough.

Admiring the little girl's independence, we usually ran to the fence and watched the tiny figure until it disappeared from sight. After about four or five performances she stopped coming to our house. Did her family move away on its horse-drawn wagon, or did she sense, with the talent of a born entertainer, that interest in her performance was waning?

Driving back to Budapest, immersed in my memories, the murmur of the Russian-made Lada sedan changed in my mind to the train's clickety-clack. There were once again no paved roads in Ujszász, the gypsy girl sang about unfulfilled love, and in Mulberry Park I scored a beautiful goal on Julius.

"Goal!"

"Goal!" yelled the kids and parents, bringing me back to the game. Goal, indeed. In uniforms, on a regulation field, with referees. What we would have given for that chance in Mulberry Park!

My appointment as a coach lasted for seven years. Nicholas and Gordon became strong players for both their soccer and their tennis teams in high school.

One day during the fall of his junior year in high school, Nicholas came home excited. "Dad, next year I'll be a football kicker on the high school team, and a real good one at that."

"Where did you get that idea?" I did not know whether to take him seriously or not.

"I just watched our high school's varsity football game. The place kickers of neither team could show a decent kick."

"Could you?" I queried.

"Why not? You know I can really boot the soccer ball. But I need help to practice."

"All right." I was skeptical, but relented with a sigh. I might as well volunteer, I thought, before I get pressured into duty. "Get that funny-shaped thing you call a ball and let's go to the field."

"Just imagine," continued Nicholas on the way to the high school, "those kids on the football teams kick the ball with their toes! No wonder their kicks are short and inaccurate."

I knew too well the boys' tendency to kick the ball with their toes. As a soccer coach, I had to deal with that problem. "How would you kick the football?"

"Just like a soccer ball, with my instep. It has to work for a football too."

Although unaware of it, Nicholas reinvented the wheel, previously invented by a fellow Hungarian-American, Pete Gogolak. I knew of Pete from platform tennis, since we entered the same tournaments a few times. I was aware that he was a football kicker in the past, but I had not yet realized the importance of his contribution in general to American football.

I learned later that Pete left Hungary as a young boy, after the revolution of 1956, with his family. In high school he realized that his skills as an excellent soccer player were not sufficiently appreciated. Switching sports, he ultimately became the person who introduced soccer-style kicking in football and became famous for that achievement as well as his results as the place kicker for the New York Giants. Now practically all place kickers use soccer-style kicking.

At the high school soccer field we paced out about thirty yards from the goal. "What do I do?" I asked Nicholas in my new position as special teams coach.

"Hold the ball with the tip of your finger and let it go just as I kick it."

"Not before?" My question came too late.

"boooom!" Lucky for me, I managed to withdraw my hand as Nicholas kicked the ball, which twirled through the air and over the crossbar of the soccer goal.

"Not bad," I remarked. "What else does a place kicker have to do?"

"Nothing. Just kick the ball over the bar."

"Doesn't it get boring? I'd stick to soccer."

"No, no," protested Nicholas. "I can be really good at this. I'd feel much better though, if a real pro could tell me what to do."

I protested. "What's the matter? Am I not holding the ball with expert hands?" Then the idea hit me. "We'll call Pete Gogolak!"

"Gogolak, the famous Giants' kicker?" Nicholas was excited. "Do you know him?"

"Not really, but he is Hungarian. That should be enough."

It was. I called Pete at his Connecticut home. Hearing my request, conveyed in Hungarian, he immediately obliged. "Come over on Sunday. I'll take a look at your boy's kicking."

Standing on the field near his magnificent house in casual attire (with the obligatory loafers without socks), Pete had only one piece of advice for Nicholas. "Just continue the natural way you are kicking now and do not listen to coaches. Chances are, they know nothing about kicking."

Sound advice it was, though it could not always be heeded. In spite of his coaches, the next season Nicholas broke his high school's record. The highlight of his senior year in high school occurred during the traditional Thanksgiving Day football match against the rival private school. Nicholas kicked the winning goal ninety-six seconds before the end of the game. Eventually, he made it to the Division I team of his university, until an injury prevented him from continuing.

Gordon, our younger son, stuck with tennis and soccer and became one of the stars of his college teams in both sports.

Settling in at his university, Nicholas called home with enthusiasm. "Dad, this is like a country club! We've got everything here, even an eighteen-hole golf course! I am glad I did not choose an inner-city school. Was your university in Budapest anything like this? Did you enjoy your college years?"

With my background in architecture and urban design, the first difference I noticed between the colleges we looked at with our sons and the Technical University of Budapest was the arrangement of buildings. It seems that in American colleges the students constantly have to be on the move from building to building, from one class to another, to the library, to the administration building, to the cafeteria. At my university in Budapest, one large three-story building housed all the facilities required for thousands of students. In the center of the building was a large space, reaching from the ground floor to the roof, with a skylight, the hub of student activities. A functional and pleasant arrangement, ideal for studies as well as for the students' community life.

Our surroundings may have been ideal, but unpleasant political events constantly overshadowed our lives at the university. The Stalinist leadership took control of the university in 1948, after I became a freshman. Had the communists been in power during the admission process, my entry might have been denied because of my political views. The Stalinist leadership made sure we could not enjoy our college years. In the evenings after our heavy schedule of classes, we were often required to participate in endless discussions praising the greatness of the Soviet Union, the Soviet system, and their leaders. Party members kept us under constant observation and reported to their leadership any small action or remark that did not meet their approval.

The university had a good tennis team. As a former junior tennis champion, I made the team easily and often escaped from political duties to the tennis courts. Sports were strongly supported by the communists, giving me the opportunity to avoid many unpleasant tasks by attending practice or tournaments.

One benefit of being on the tennis team occurred during May Day parades. I was allowed to express my everlasting gratitude to the Great Stalin and his Hungarian cronies during that communist holiday with my tennis team. I did not have to assemble at seven in the morning with my classmates and march for five or six hours in order to salute the dignitaries on the stand near Stalin's statue. Instead, dressed in our tennis uniforms, our "elite" group enjoyed priority treatment and managed to complete the entire march in a couple of hours. Best of all, we were in good company and did not have to put up with the communist leaders of our respective classes. Once to ourselves, members of the team could forget about the political turmoil. We felt free. On one occasion we wanted to share our comradeship with Zoli, a friend who was not so fortunate. He was having difficulties with his political leaders and badly needed a break.

Traveling for a weekend tournament to the lovely city of Pécs, we invited Zoli, who knew nothing about tennis, to tag along as a substitute player. In that capacity, Zoli would also enjoy free room and board at the local university. Everything went well until our opponents graciously offered to set Zoli up with a match.

"There is another court available," the opposing team's captain told us. "We can provide a substitute player too, and have another match."

Somehow Zoli managed to excuse himself from play without arousing suspicion. He had a more difficult task when asked to referee one of the matches. Not knowing even how to keep score, Zoli almost had to reveal that he was not a tennis player, but in the last minute he found a solution.

"We'll do this in a gentlemanly manner," he announced, sitting in the umpire's chair. "You players will make the calls and announce the score. I interfere only if I disagree with your calls."

Zoli sweated it out, suffering for his free room and board. Needless to say, he always found the players' calls correct. We had a good laugh about the entire affair later, but Zoli never asked to join us on a tour again.

My university's tennis courts did not resemble a country club in any way as did the sport facilities at Nicholas's school. However, as tournament players, my teammates and I received free court time and equipment and, most important, were relieved from many political activities and endless discussions on the merits of communism. For this privilege, I was grateful. But I was mistaken when I thought that my political problems at school were solved. The worst that communism would deal me while I was a student was yet to come.

6

EDUCATED
UNDER STALIN

"What specifically was so bad about living in a communist country?" asked Gordon. "You had a good education, opportunity to play sports."

"That's right," said Nicholas, "and you were able to afford such luxuries as frequently going to the theater and opera."

My boys had seen communist Hungary only as visitors, and during the years of "goulash" communism, a liberalized version of the system. Life was quite different when Stalin reigned in the Soviet Union and his friend, the Soviet citizen Mátyás Rákosi, ruled Hungary.

I was lucky to be admitted to the Technical University of Budapest before the communists took control of the administration and the admission policy of that great institution. The worst effects of the Stalinist period in Hungary started during my first year as a student of architecture. What should have been the best years of my life turned at times into a nightmare.

Under pressure of the Soviet occupying forces, the short-lived postwar democratic political system rapidly changed to a dictatorship of the proletariat, on paper, but in reality to a dictatorship whose beneficiaries were only the top leadership of the country and the Soviet Union.

Personal cult was introduced, with hero worship taking center stage on the political arena. The greatest of all, of course, was Stalin. Rákosi, leader of the Hungarian communist party became the "fountainhead of all wisdom." We were to mention his name only with the utmost respect.

The Russians inundated Hungary with propaganda proclaiming their superiority. We were expected to worship the Soviet system. All over the country new monuments were erected to the Soviets. In the City Park of

Budapest a huge statue of Stalin replaced a church. The square in front of the statue became the place where leaders of the communist party viewed the marching crowd during May Day parades.

First the factories and large farms were confiscated without compensation, and then every business and piece of real estate, with the exception of a few small stores, workshops, and dwelling units with fewer than six rooms, was seized by the communist powers.

Just taking people's property did not satisfy the communists. Those with wealth before nationalization were branded "class alien," enemies of socialism and the working class. According to communist theory, the class struggle had to be kept alive, always finding new groups of people to hate and chastise.

As management of industries and farms fell into the hands of communist charlatans, and a large portion of goods found its way to the Great Socialist Homeland, the Soviet Union, the stores were less and less well stocked. Finally, shortages became so acute that food coupons had to be introduced in a country that had traditionally exported farm products. With their unique logic, the communists blamed the shortages on "sabotage" and on people who hoarded unnecessary amounts of merchandise. The police conducted random searches of private homes, and anyone with more than a few days' supply of food faced severe punishment. The "criminal" behavior of individuals apprehended for economic and political "crimes" was publicized to frighten the population.

Meanwhile, leaders of the Communist Party were not suffering from shortages. Special stores catered to their exclusive needs, where they could pick up merchandise in chauffeur-driven limousines at reduced prices.

A political cleanup started in places of work and learning. Real and imaginary opponents of communism had to go to make room for the new chosen class. In more severe cases people were arrested and convicted on trumped-up charges. Luckier victims only lost their jobs or were demoted. Well-known people were subjected to widely publicized trials. One of the most famous of these trials was that of Cardinal József Mindszenty. The cardinal, an outspoken and unyielding person, had been persecuted and jailed previously by the fascists. Now the communists arrested him. Before his trial, he was forced to take mind-altering drugs and was severely tortured for weeks. The cardinal was sentenced to life imprisonment for "treason." Rákosi also purged some of his own party's members to ensure that he had no rival in the country. In 1951, La'szló Rajk, a fellow leader of the party, was sentenced to death and hanged.

No one knew when the secret police might arrive at the doorstep. Our family had a scare one day when two official-looking men rang the doorbell. They bluntly requested entry and demanded that we engage in political conversation. This sort of political "education" was often forced on people whom the communists suspected of having greater than average resistance to their ideas.

"Do you agree with the party's policy on foreign affairs?" one of the intruders demanded to know, and continued with similar questions.

Of course, it would have been suicidal to disagree with the official line. I was worried about the reason for the sudden political discussion the two men forced on us. We were relieved when we found out that all these men wanted were subscriptions to the Communist Party's newspaper. They were simply using their version of salesmanship—intimidation.

Attending a technical university had distinct advantages. With the hasty industrialization of the country the communists created a great need for technical experts. At our university, political pasts and loyalties were handled a little more leniently than at schools where students were preparing, for example, to be lawyers or teachers. Attila, my friend from high school, who studied for his bachelor of arts degree at another university, learned the severity of political control there the hard way. After the Ministry of Education ordered the closing of all private dormitories, including the one where he stayed, Attila found a home in our apartment.

One day Attila came home worried. "Csaba, I may be in trouble," he said. "A colleague of mine told me that two strangers have been inquiring about me."

There was nothing Attila could do but wait and hope. His hopes were in vain. Early one morning, a few weeks later, two plainclothes secret police came to arrest him. Attila stood in the vestibule of the apartment, dumfounded, scared, with an embarrassed smile on his face. "There must be a mistake," he pleaded. "I didn't do anything."

The smile on Attila's face obviously irritated one of the husky men.

"Just get moving," he demanded. "Soon you will not smile."

He was right. My friend was tortured for three days. Finally, favorable evidence and his inability to incriminate himself convinced Attila's tormentors that he was not involved in the writing of anticommunist literature they discovered on university grounds.

The torture was quite sophisticated: electrical shocks, deprivation of sleep, force-feeding with salt. These methods do not leave marks. When his torturers beat him, they hit only the soles of his feet, where physical abuse cannot usually be detected.

One night when his tormentors left Attila alone for a while, a young guard took pity on him and offered encouragement to stay strong. "You are one of the lucky ones," the guard said. "They are much tougher on some of the other prisoners."

Indeed, my friend was lucky. He was kicked out of the secret police headquarters with only a severe warning. "All right, you didn't do anything this time. However, if you as much as whisper a word about what happened here, we'll take care of you. And don't forget, we'll be watching you closely."

Attila did try to keep to himself what happened at the secret police headquarters, but his painful limping and nightmares were telltale signs. We knew better than to inquire; he told the full story only years later.

The communists used informers to probe for evidence they could use to weed out opposition. But despite the weakness of human nature, it was impossible to find enough volunteers for that despicable function. They turned to coercive methods to force people to do their dirty work. The secret police took one friend of mine to their headquarters and gave him forty-eight hours to accept their offer. His choice was either to spy on his colleagues or go to jail on trumped-up charges. My friend was torn between his conscience and the desire to be free, if one can call the life of a forced informer free. Not being able to lower himself to yield to the communists, my friend said good-bye to his boss, the chief engineer of his company.

Hearing the reason for my friend's farewell, the chief engineer took a different view. He was delighted. "Please, please accept the secret police's offer," he exclaimed. "We'd love to know who the informer is—especially if he is a person like you!"

My friend became an "informer." His consolation for his monthly trips to secret police headquarters was that he managed to keep all his colleagues out of trouble.

Politics in my university class of about one hundred students was controlled by a small group headed by a fellow named Mishka. He initiated endless discussions on the greatness of socialism and demanded that we prostrate ourselves by praising the party's leaders and the terrible communist social and economic system. This humiliating psychological ploy used by the communists contributed to the buildup of anger and frustration in the general population.

One day Mishka called a meeting of our study group and announced that someone among us committed a terrible sin. Steve Botond (who is now practicing architecture in Nevada) had dared to tell a joke derogatory to the Soviet system. Despite the harsh penalties for telling them, political jokes were always plentiful in Budapest.

The charge against Steve was serious. We were afraid that he might be taken away by the secret police and possibly sentenced to many years in prison, just as our classmate Leslie Pályi had been a few months earlier. Leslie was lucky to survive the cruel treatment he received during interrogation. Even when the secret police were through with the torture, they made him "relax" for weeks in a room filled with water waist-high before transferring him to a jail. Leslie was liberated from prison only by the Hungarian Revolution, about six years after his incarceration. Eventually he also ended up in the United States.

The meeting continued, and Mishka seemed very upset. He continued: "Steve Botond insulted the great Soviet hero Michurin, the miracle scientist of agriculture."

It was a relief to hear that the charge was only the telling of a Michurin joke. At worst, Steve would be kicked out of the university or suspended. Had he insulted the Great Stalin or his local crony Rákosi, Steve's fate would have been sealed.

Michurin was the Russian horticulturist to whom the theory was attributed that sudden changes, "jumps," can occur in nature, replacing evolution; thus the genetics of plants can easily be altered to fit different climatic conditions. Michurin's motto was shown on signs throughout the city: "We do not beg Nature for gifts!" On that basis, horticulturists were assigned to impossible tasks such as growing oranges in the Hungarian climate.

Stalin embraced and ordered the official acceptance of Michurin's theory because he wanted to prove that sudden changes can be achieved in nature, including human behavior. This latter thesis was crucial to Stalin, because the communist economic system obviously could not (and did not) work with human nature as it is. Without the incentives of a market-oriented economy that rewards people according to their achievements, the Soviet system was doomed to failure, unless a change in human behavior would take place.

I looked at Steve's worried face. "With a little help," I thought, "he might get out of this one." What could I do? Then suddenly an idea hit me. Risky, but it should work. "Come on, Mishka," I said smiling. "Those Michurin jokes are not disrespectful; rather they express the popularity of the great Soviet scientist. I heard a Michurin joke too."

Noticing the surprised expression on my colleagues' faces, I almost chickened out, but in the end gathered up the courage to continue. "Michurin crossed the corn with the typewriter. The result? Eating the corn, at the end of each row the bell rings. Now isn't that cute? Nothing malicious."

Nobody laughed. After a little while, however, one of my classmates repeated my remark. "That's right. Nothing malicious in that joke."

A few more students nodded in approval. Others just stared, but their eyes revealed how disgusted they were about the entire discussion. I eagerly watched Mishka's face since now my future was jeopardized too. "If he wants Steve kicked out," I told myself, "he will have to demand my dismissal from the university too."

After a long pause, with the air full of tension, Mishka yielded. We got away with a long lecture about socialist behavior and respect, and a warning.

The small group of Stalinists often made our lives miserable. There was no recourse against them except exclusion from our private circles. They were outcasts, and they felt it. Ivan, a less extreme communist, cracked under the pressure. At a political meeting we all had to attend, he bitterly complained about the division between the communist leaders and the rest of the class.

"Why don't you ever include us in your friendly get-togethers?" he queried.

Nobody responded and nobody was moved, except his communist

friends, who summarily kicked Ivan out of the party. A public announcement of such a division in a great socialist society was unacceptable.

While I was studying for my architectural degree, the communist government, with Russian guidance, was concentrating on investing in heavy industry while ignoring consumer needs. Hungary had to follow the lead of a country that was backward not only in its social but also in its economic system. The Russians' lack of experience in dealing with simple technical things indicated how primitive Soviet society must have been. Considering the Russian example, for instance, certificates were required to operate automatic elevators in apartment buildings. Certificates were provided upon completion of a test!

Replacing our Western outlook with Russian influence and culture was a main goal of the Soviet system. Schools shifted from teaching Western languages. Everybody had to study Russian. Russian books, movies, plays were forced upon the population. Anything and everything Russian was wonderful and superior. Contact with the Western world was prohibited. The borders were sealed, permission to travel was almost unattainable, even to other communist countries. Had the Soviet system lasted much longer, Hungarians would have lost much of their national identity. The Russians' effort was not exactly ethnic cleansing, but it was a first step toward it.

With the elaborate communist bureaucratic administration requiring additional workers in the capital, Budapest's urban population rapidly swelled, creating housing shortages. Following the Soviet example concerning the provision of living accommodations, families were forced to share apartments. Copying Russian blueprints, apartment buildings were planned that provided only community bathroom facilities. Overcrowding was not the only effect of the lack of adequate housing. The Stalinists solved their own housing needs with usual cruelty and blatant disregard for the rights of innocent human beings.

My girlfriend, Margo, called me. "Csaba, we're on the list," she said.

"What list?" I was studying hard and had not been keeping up with current events.

"Haven't you heard about the deportations?"

I could hardly believe my ears. Apparently, the communists had found a solution to the housing needs. Or at least to *their* housing needs. They started to deport "undesirable" people. Party faithful took possession of the deportees' apartments, along with the former inhabitants' belongings. Tens of thousands of families found themselves on trucks after only a few hours of notice, heading toward kulaks' farms. Kulaks, "enemies of the socialist system," were those farmers who owned more land than what the communists would tolerate without repercussions. The farmers had to provide room and board to the deported families, who in turn were required to labor in the fields. The deportees' movements were restricted to within a few miles of the farm.

Margo's grandfather, who died well before World War II, was a tradesman. Through hard work, he established his own workshop that in time became a small factory. In the eyes of the communists, members of his family were capitalists. They—including the four grandchildren, the smallest of whom was only three years old—were enemies of the people. Fortunately, Margo's father found out about their impending fate in advance from a friend who had inside information, and he was able to rescue a few valuables from their apartment before the actual date of deportation.

When the news of deportations hit I was near the end of my studies and believed that the hardest part of political pressure was over. Instead of getting better, some of the darkest days of the dictatorship were on their way. A large segment of the population, including our family, lived in intense fear for months. In addition to Margo's family, a number of my friends and a distant aunt were earmarked for deportation. My aunt's "crime" was that her husband, who died around 1930, was a high-ranking army officer during World War I.

Margo and I were devastated. The Iron Curtain tightly sealed the country's borders. Escape to the West would have been very dangerous and almost impossible at that time. Help could come only from within the country, but there was nowhere to turn. Not knowing the exact day of deportation, we found every remaining day before that fateful act to be both a torture and a gift. Perhaps even worse than the actual misdeeds was the sense of helplessness, feeling totally at the mercy of unscrupulous people. There was no recourse, no hope; we felt like puppets dancing as the communists pulled the strings.

The last day I saw Margo before her deportation, we took the cog railway into the picturesque hills of Buda. Leaving the terminal station, Margo and I climbed up the gentle slopes quietly, but we could not enjoy the beautiful panoramic view darkened by angry clouds. Little fireflies danced grotesquely as we sat down in a secluded place. Margo placed her head in my lap, her face wet with tears. She knew this could be our farewell.

Walking down toward the city at sundown, a myriad of lightning bugs flickered in front of us aimlessly. Their wavering lights did not illuminate the way but died quickly as we descended into the ever-darkening valley.

7

SOCIALIST PRODUCTIVITY

There they nested, on the top of a chimney, as I had promised my boys. One of the storks clattered loudly and spread its wings.

"Aren't they afraid of people?" asked Gordon, who adores animals and was surprised to see that storks choose to live in the company of people, rather than in the wild.

It is heartwarming to see these beautiful birds in some of the Hungarian villages. The storks and their nests complemented the vernacular architecture of single-story houses with reed-thatched roofs in the village we visited near Lake Balaton.

In America one sees storks only on pictures or television, since these birds are not indigenous to that part of the world. Most Americans do not see swallows, either, although those feathered creatures are native to the United States. In Hungary, swallows favor people's proximity even more than storks. In the spring, arriving after a long trip from Africa, swallows promptly start building nests on the inside walls of barns, covered porches, terraces, even on blank walls of houses that have sufficient overhangs for some protection from the elements. Their nests, glued to the wall and built with great craftsmanship, could easily be reached; still, the swallows are not afraid of human intervention.

A few days after arriving in Budapest with my boys and visiting the village containing the storks, Gordon approached my sister. "Can we go and see the swallows?" he asked.

"Of course!" Ildikó said. It was in the early 1980s, and, having received amnesty for her behavior during the revolution, Ildikó, a horticulturist, was manager of a nursery in the outskirts of Budapest. The nursery grew mainly flowers and plants for the city's parks. One autumn they demolished an old barn that was also the home of a swallow couple. The next spring the swallows arrived and found no barn, circled around for a while, then flew into one of the offices through an open window. Before the rightful inhabitants of the workplace could think twice about what was going on, the swallows started building their nest, working feverishly. From that day on, rain or shine, hot or cold, a window of that office had to be kept open from spring till early September, when the swallows depart with their extended family. During the summer, human voices, the clattering of typewriters, and the chirping of chicks harmonize.

Gordon could hardly wait to see the swallow family. "May I feed the babies?" he asked.

"No," said Ildikó. "Whatever nature provides them has to suffice. Besides, the swallows probably would not like the idea, anyway. Although I have some food I would like to dispose of in a useful way."

"What is it?" I inquired.

"Russian bread. Dark as chocolate, and hardly digestible. Compliments of the Russian commandant in the nearby camp."

Representative of the bankrupt Soviet economy was the quality of their agricultural products. The occupying Russian forces received provisions according to the standards of their country and were strongly discouraged from mixing with the local population. No wonder. The Russians did not want their citizens to see the vast difference in the standard of living between the Soviet Union and Hungary. By this time, reformed communists had taken over the government in Hungary. They followed the Russians' lead only to the extent that was unavoidable. For this reason, the economic situation in this unwilling satellite country was far superior to the Soviets' in their own country.

Ildikó had an insight into the Russians' poverty, through her official connection to them. On Soviet holidays and other special occasions the Russian commandant asked Ildikó's company for flowers to decorate their bleak barracks. In return, the Russians sent over their enlisted men to provide free manual labor. The soldiers worked hard all day and were happy to do so just for receiving a decent meal.

Occasionally, the commandant wanted to express his appreciation to Ildikó for making the business arrangements and, upon her visits to the camp, gave her little gifts he believed to be valuable, such as a loaf of bread.

At one time, when the commandant felt especially indebted, he sent the other officers out of his office and opened the safe. There it was, securely hidden, an entire loaf of *white* bread. He cut a large slice, wrapped it in newspaper and, beaming, handed this precious gift to Ildikó. "Just for you. I, as the commandant, am entitled to some white bread," he said proudly.

Ildikó was touched, not by the value of the gift but by the realization of the Russians' grave poverty. This commandant's behavior was quite different from that of the arrogant invading-liberating Soviet soldiers in 1945.

The episode with the Soviet commandant clearly illustrated the extent of the communist economy's failure. Fallacies of the Marxist economic theories became obvious to me when I learned about them at my university. We did not have to waste too much effort studying the subject of "Capitalist and Socialist Political Economy," but the little time we did spend on these topics was sufficient for me to realize the absurdity of the Marxist-Leninist economic theory, which is based more on false political ideas and hate for people with means than on sound facts.

Upon graduation, still during Stalinist times, I soon had the opportunity to experience firsthand the effects of communist economic ideology. The first disappointment came when school authorities issued my diploma. With it I received my Personal Identification Booklet. That document contained, in addition to personal data, a section for my work history.

I was dismayed to see that my first place of employment had already been entered in the booklet. Neither my employer nor I was consulted. The communists believed that in a nonmarket-oriented economy nobody had to be concerned with a "minor" detail like that. Another demoralizing rule was that a worker could change jobs only with his employer's permission. If someone gave notice for termination of employment without his superiors' consent, it was noted in his booklet and he could not be hired by another company. This seemed to me nothing more than a modern version of slave labor.

I decided to protest to the university's authorities. "I have a job offer I would like to accept. I never heard of this company to which you assigned me. Why should I work there?"

"That's where the socialist economy needs you" was the explanation. Naturally, the socialist economy needed the party members at choice positions with better pay and advancement possibilities. It was not important whether or not they were suitable to fulfill their duties. Mishka, who had failed a number of subjects and had to repeat a year of schooling, was one of those who obtained a higher-paying position. Though disappointed in my assignment to a small construction company, I had to resign myself to the communists' unfair practices.

The much publicized and praised five-year economic plans demanded the rigid following of instructions dreamed up in a central planning office. Possibilities for individual incentives were minimal. No matter whether it made sense or not, THE PLAN and all its arbitrary requirements had to be fulfilled.

Often strange, unproductive, stupid actions had to be taken. At a construction project where I was involved in my first job as a professional architect, we had to order stone at an unreasonably high cost from a faraway place. The blueprints showed expensive, thick stone walls. This method of construction made sense at the time of planning because there was a quarry operation near the site. Now exhausted of its material, the quarry had been closed down, but the buildings still had to be built of stone, doubling the expense. After all, that's the way the plans were drawn.

When I protested to my superiors about the waste, the answer was always the same: "We cannot make any changes to the plan."

The rigidity of central planning methods cost the country dearly. An extreme case was seen throughout the city's parks, where occasionally the watering of lawns continued during rains. Plans for water consumption had to be met, regardless of circumstances.

Perhaps the elimination of a true relationship between value and price caused the greatest damage to the socialist economies. After a few years of rigid planning that disregarded market forces, nobody knew the real value of products; they could only be guessed by following prices in the Western countries.

At the time when I started working, most of us still had good work ethics. People cared and tried to produce goods or services in an economical, rational way. Years of unsuccessful efforts changed all that. After a while, professionals and workers alike just shrugged their shoulders and did what the plans demanded.

Under these chaotic economic circumstances I achieved a major capitalist goal seldom reached in a communist country. I made it to the floor of the Hungarian Stock Exchange. With the stock market eliminated, the large trading floor of the building was temporarily converted to an indoor tennis court, reserved for tournament players. With my teammates we quoted numbers there, but they related not to stock or bond prices but to the scores of our matches.

Heavy industrialization created a shortage of technical experts. Compensation at work was meager, but those who could obtain permission to leave their employment could easily find jobs elsewhere. My goal was to find employment in a place where the communist leaders were not die-hard Stalinists but at worst only misled individuals who joined the party with good intentions. It was possible to achieve that goal, since only a very small number of people in the country followed Moscow's lead with enthusiasm.

My first effort toward obtaining a job in pleasant surroundings was successful only temporarily. I had the good fortune of obtaining permission to leave my first job and joined a prestigious architectural design firm. I enjoyed my work and also the office's location. Our windows faced the Danube River with a view of the Castle Hill of Buda. Our director was a moderate communist, who for that reason could not keep his position. "Comrade" Seny became our boss. He was not a Stalinist, just an unscrupulous careerist. He proved that despite full employment, job security did not apply to everybody. After one week on the job, Comrade Seny asked all the architects to report on the status of our projects. Having collected the data, he summarily dismissed from employment those of us whom he found politically undesirable, with a few weeks notice. He hired others who were either his friends or politically more desirable people.

I was surprised to see Seny again after the revolution, in December, 1956, on the streets of Vienna.

"What are you doing here, 'Comrade' Seny?" I asked with considerable sarcasm.

"Come on, don't call me comrade," he pleaded, somewhat embarrassed. He was not too embarrassed, though, to tell me that, as a "refugee" fleeing communist oppression, he was busy collecting relief from the various charitable organizations.

During the early 1950s, the Communist Party, having consolidated its power in the country, turned toward cleansing itself by purging all those who were not inclined to provide 100 percent subordination to Soviet interests. Communist leaders who felt a greater responsibility toward the Hungarian people than to the Soviet Union were tried and executed or jailed.

Only Stalin's death in 1953 brought relief—as well as great improvements to the Soviet Union and the satellite countries. Under Georgy Malenkov, Stalin's successor, the tide turned in the fight between the Stalinist and Nationalist factions of the Communist Party. The much-hated Mátyás Rákosi in Hungary was replaced by Imre Nagy, who later became the people's choice for leadership during the revolution. The new government eased the political pressure and took promising steps to improve the standard of living.

During these times I found another position at an office where the director and personnel manager were former workers and, although believers of communist ideology, had good intentions. They managed to "lose" the file, with its politically damaging contents, that followed me from one place of work to another and replaced it with favorable material.

The Iron Curtain still existed, but travel between communist countries became possible under special circumstances. Grandmother was elated that her brother, Uncle Lajos, was able to visit us from Transylvania.

Although siblings, Grandmother and Uncle Lajos found each other late in life. Grandmother discovered as an adult that she had been adopted, but without official papers. In the nineteenth century there was not much need in everyday life for birth certificates and other documents. Only when preparing for her marriage did Grandmother need a birth certificate. On the document her real name appeared. Her natural mother was a poor peasant girl, who later married and had a son.

Grandmother, heartbroken by this news, continued to consider herself as the daughter of her adoptive parents. Years later, when a letter arrived from a man who claimed to be her brother, she wanted nothing to do with that "stranger." In time, however, Grandmother and Uncle Lajos met. The siblings immediately took a liking to each other and got along very well, despite the great difference in their upbringing. Their personalities must have been very similar; even their handwriting looked almost the same.

The crack in the internal Iron Curtain opened borders between the communist countries and allowed us to enjoy Uncle Lajos's company. The desirable political changes did not last long. Just when people were beginning to feel relief from the grips of a ruthless dictatorship, Nikita Khrushchev replaced Malenkov in the Soviet Union. The Russian pressure intensified, and conservative communists again took control in Hungary.

The Stalinists wanted to regain power, not only in support of their political convictions but also to enjoy their preferential status with its many material advantages. Political theories about the rule of the working class and equality of all did not stop them from awarding themselves privileges beyond belief. During Stalinist times, they confiscated all of the summer cottages of two resort towns along Lake Balaton without compensation. One of these cottages was owned by Margo's father. A few months before their deportation he received a notice from the government that his cottage, along with everybody else's in that town, would be used for government purposes, for an "indefinite period of time." Use of the two summer resort towns was restricted to the communist leadership and their families. The entire area was fenced in and heavily guarded.

The family of my friend Rudi Kriegler, with whom I later escaped from communist Hungary, had a similar experience. They owned a four-room house in a desirable one-family district in the hills of Buda. Because of its size, their house was not nationalized. However, the property was located in a district favored by the communist rulers; therefore it was also taken over for an "indefinite period of time." Rudi's family had to be content with obtaining the right to move into a small two-room rental apartment in a densely populated, less desirable neighborhood.

With the return of Stalinists to key leadership positions, the political situation became volatile. Fearing the revival of Stalinist times with its rampant deportations, discrimination, food shortages, poverty, and jailing and harassment of so many innocent people, the population became desperate. Legal and illegal discussion groups mushroomed, and confrontation became inevitable. The large-scale demonstrations and revolution that followed the general discontent was the first major step in shaking the entire communist system in Europe.

8

FREEDOM OR DEATH

Fortunately, the World Trade Center's 110-story building withstood the blast; it did not collapse. The terrorist act, however, that aimed at the total destruction of that structure was a clear reminder that some unhappy political and national groups may want to reach their goals by urban guerrilla warfare.

The bombing of the World Trade Center prompted Nicholas to ask, "Were there Hungarian guerrillas fighting during the revolution against the communists?"

Nicholas's question made me think. Why have there been no Hungarian guerrillas or international terrorists? Usually when a nation is deprived or believed to be deprived of freedom by other nations, a few members engage in some sort of guerrilla warfare or terrorism. The Middle East is a prime example. In Europe, the Basques commit terrorist acts, wanting an independent country or autonomy; the Irish attack the English to achieve the unification of Ireland; the Austrians in South Tirol obtained concessions from the ruling Italians through a guerrilla movement; the Croatians committed skyjacking in order to bring the world's attention to the fact that their country at that time was controlled by the Serbians. But Hungarians are not known for either guerrilla or terrorist activities and fought the revolution without the use of such tactics.

To understand the significance of the fact that no guerrilla activities are tied to Hungarian movements, one has to realize that about one-third of Hungarians live in neighboring countries, most of them under conditions that aim to erase their national identity, maintained there for over a thousand years. In Central Europe Hungarians represent the largest number of minorities in foreign countries.

I remember a scene that occurred a few days after the outbreak of the revolution. Russian soldiers were getting out of their tank near our apartment building. It was a peaceful intersection, but only a few blocks away from the core of the fighting. Neither there nor at any other place did the revolutionary forces shoot at unsuspecting soldiers who would have been easy targets. I do not know the reason. Is it in the Hungarian character?

On the same day that I watched the Russian soldiers walking around their tanks unharmed, the Soviet-trained secret police demonstrated quite different ethics. They met unsuspecting demonstrators with gunfire at various locations of Budapest, causing many deaths and injuries. Many of us who did not take up arms continued to demonstrate on the streets, despite the dangers. I met a determined group on József Boulevard a few days after the outbreak of the revolution.

"Freedom or death! Freedom or death!" they chanted, carrying a Hungarian flag, with the red star torn out of its center, marching by the Soviet tank and its soldiers.

At this particular location the Russians were just watching the demonstrators without realizing what was going on. This lack of understanding on the part of the invading forces was a characteristic feature of the revolution during the first few days.

I approached one of the marchers. "Where are you heading?"

"To the Parliament!"

"No, no, don't!" I protested. "I have just come from there; the secret police slaughtered thousands."

I was lucky that day. The secret police started shooting indiscriminately just as I was approaching the Parliament area after a meeting with my company's revolutionary committee. Rapid gunfire interrupted the peaceful demonstrators' chanting. Russian tanks joined in, and explosions of their shells shook the buildings all around me. It was not clear to me at whom the Russian tanks were firing in the confusion; they had no clear understanding of what was going on.

Just as suddenly as it started, the shooting stopped. Screams and cries replaced the sounds of explosions. Men, women, and children appeared, running; some of them with blood-soaked clothes. Many died, and many suffered crippling injuries in front of the Parliament building that was to symbolize that the will of the people is to prevail.

"Oh my God!" screamed a woman. "They're killing everybody."

Hearing my report of the tragic events that occurred at the Parliament, the marchers along József Boulevard just shrugged their shoulders and continued on their way.

"Freedom or death!"

The demonstrators' fearless, desperate attitude was characteristic during the revolution that erupted in the fall of 1956. People rejected the actions of the Russian citizen Rákosi and his right-hand man Ernő Gerő to regain total control of the Communist Party in Hungary. Hundreds of thousands of people demonstrated against their effort and demanded the reappointment of the moderate Imre Nagy.

The largest demonstration occurred prior to the hostilities, on October 23, 1956, in front of the Parliament building. In the large square in front of the monumental building there was enough room for tens of thousands of people. I went there by myself, not with an organized group, to demand with the other demonstrators the appearance of Imre Nagy. We wanted his reassurance that he and not the hated and feared Stalinists would lead the country.

While waiting for Nagy to appear, I engaged in conversation with my fellow demonstrators. What an exhilarating experience it was to discuss openly and frankly the country's problems and future with strangers, without fear of the secret police!

"I hope Nagy will show," I said.

"Why do you want Nagy?" argued a young woman who looked like a college student. "He is a communist just like the others."

"Under the circumstances he is the best we can hope for," commented a middle-aged man. "Nagy proved during the past few years that he is all right. The Russians wouldn't allow a greater change than what he'd represent."

"Will they allow even as much as Nagy taking over?" I questioned. "I am not sure at all."

"There he is," yelled the young woman, pointing toward the Parliament building where Nagy appeared on a platform, accompanied by a number of people. The crowd cheered.

"I wonder whether his entourage consists of his aides, or if they are secret police, to keep him under control," I remarked.

"Good question," said the middle-aged man. "Maybe we'll know soon."

As the applause died down, Nagy started to speak. "Comrades!"

We booed so loudly that it convinced Nagy—or those with him—that the tone of the impromptu speech would have to be changed.

"My friends!"

We were overjoyed. The crowd went wild. After about eight years of communist rule, finally we were addressed properly.

I do not remember anything memorable about the speech, but it seemed that by allowing Nagy to address the demonstrators, the Stalinist leaders accepted him as the future leader of the country.

My jubilation turned into concern when the news spread on the square that fighting broke out in the eighth district, near my home. While still listening to Imre Nagy, we learned that demonstrators at the radio station requested that their demands be announced over the air waves. At first the Stalinists sent army troops to disperse the demonstrators. Instead, the soldiers sided with the people. Unable to control either the police or the armed forces, the Stalinists ordered the secret police to use force. Only they were willing to shoot at the unarmed demonstrators.

Some of the people listening to Nagy decided to rush to the radio station; others preferred to stay near the Parliament. At this juncture, participants in the demonstration had to decide for themselves whether to fight for freedom only by peaceful means or also by force.

To me, the armed intervention of the secret police was a signal that the Stalinists and the Russians would not give up Hungary. Standing in the square that was named after Lajos Kossuth, leader of the 1848 revolution against the Hapsburgs (which was defeated by the Russian army), I was concerned that now, just as then, Hungary might be at the mercy of great powers, without help. On one of the sculptures on the square were carved the words of the poet Sándor Petőfi, who described the nation's fight in that nineteenth-century revolution:

From the mountains to the lower Danube,
In the storm with painful cries and no friends,
Covered with wounds and cuts in the midst of fight,
All by himself, the Hungarian stands.

Since the secret police were unable to control the demonstrators, the following day Russian troops that were stationed in the country under the

Warsaw Pact intervened. The Russians were not well prepared for their task. In a conventional war, it is clear who is fighting whom. During the first days of the revolution, the Soviet soldiers often could not determine who their enemy was. Some of the demonstrators confused the Russians by greeting them and joining their troops. Bewildered by their order to fight "fascist invaders," the Russians, finding only peacefully demonstrating civilians, refused to fire. But inevitably, at certain locations the Soviet troops clashed with Hungarians.

Based on their previous experience in East Germany and Poland, the Soviet leadership believed that the mere appearance of tanks would frighten the population into submission. They paid dearly for their miscalculation. The fighting escalated; the few Hungarian soldiers stationed in the city were joined by many young people, mostly in their teens and early twenties. Soon dozens of disabled Russian tanks and dead bodies covered the major arteries of a section of Budapest. Many buildings also suffered considerable damage and a number of Hungarians lost their lives during the battles. Presence of Soviet troops, however, did not always lead to military actions. In parts of the city, demonstrations continued peacefully.

As a member of my company's revolutionary committee, I enjoyed seeing how some of the communist leaders suddenly changed. Our company's communist director made a pitiful and comical scene as he forcefully banged on the table with his fists, supporting our revolutionary committee and democratic ideas.

"We want free elections!" he demanded more loudly then any of the true revolutionaries.

I was heading home after one of our meetings, along the main artery that circled the city's central area. (József Boulevard is a part of this ring.) I passed by a hotel near the Western Train Station. A large red star, the symbol of communism, decorated the hotel, attached to the wall at the top floor. A woman leaned out of a window, with one hand holding onto a man's arm and the other hammering the red star until all its pieces fell to the ground. A large crowd watched happily and cheered.

On the other side of the roadway a Russian tank aimed its gun at the woman, but the soldiers dared not or did not want to shoot. An onlooker knocked on the tank and offered cigarettes to the Russian, who cautiously emerged from under the protective hatch of the tank. He seemed totally bewildered, unable to distinguish between friend and foe.

Farther along the boulevard people greeted the Russian soldiers with flowers, befriended them, and rode on the top of their tanks. These soldiers' confusion was even greater.

Nearing József Boulevard, I passed Budapest's busiest intersection, the place where I had sold cigarettes on the black market as an adolescent after the war. Now eager hands were chopping pieces from Stalin's statue with relentless hammering. The hated dictator's monument had been dragged to that location so that more people could see his desecration. Rather than pedophiles approaching unsuspecting youngsters, the dangerous elements of that area now were Russian tanks and snipers of the secret police, who occasionally shot at the demonstrators from nearby rooftops.

Approaching my neighborhood, I almost became a fatality of the fighting myself. Seeing a tank in the distance, I switched to the side streets. I felt that this precaution was necessary because our apartment was at the edge of the area where fierce fighting took place. While I made my way toward our apartment the Russian tank moved much closer to our building. As I emerged from the side street to József Boulevard from which the door of our building opened, the tank's turret moved in my direction. For a split second I froze, then ran as fast as I could toward the safety of the street behind our building.

It is amazing how the length of a short block can grow to such a long distance. "This is it," I thought, while trying to run faster. "At least if I had a weapon I could die shooting back. No, I am better off running. This way I have a chance."

My heart pounding, sweat pouring off my face, not necessarily as the result of the sudden exercise, I turned the corner.

"I made it," I thought. "Mother won't have to bury me." At that moment a shell swished by and exploded with a loud bang on the strong masonry wall of a building in the side street. My knees shaking, I realized that the euphoria about my survival had been premature. There was no confusion about the intentions of this tank.

Aside from the blast and a good scare, no harm came to me. In the back street I was safe once I moved away from the corner. In the city,

Russian tanks dared to drive only along the wide roadways since Molotov cocktails could be thrown very effectively from the windows on narrow streets. Unable to approach the front door of our apartment building, I climbed in someone's window at the back of the building. Hurrying up to the second floor, I was wondering about who was at my home, safe. Now five of us shared the apartment: Mother, Grandmother, Ildikó and her husband of two years, and me. My father had passed away earlier that year, in the spring.

As it turned out, only my mother and grandmother were home, in the kitchen, whose window faced the inner courtyard.

"How did you get home?" asked Mother. "We saw Russian tanks on the Boulevard; that's why we're not in the living room."

"We just heard an explosion a few minutes ago. Do you know where it happened?" asked Grandmother.

"Not too far away," I answered without mentioning my frightening experience, but I was concerned about Ildikó and her husband. I needn't have worried. They had more sense than I; they came home after dark.

During the next few days conditions remained chaotic. In parts of Budapest the fighting never stopped. In others demonstrations continued, and in some areas preparations took place for a new, democratic system.

These days were very difficult for me. I was among those who could not believe that the Soviets would tolerate a free Hungary and anticipated the worst. But my reservations about the revolution's future did not stop me from doing what I believed was morally right. I was elected a member of the revolutionary committee of my office, spoke up in meetings, participated in demonstrations, and joined one of the new opposition parties. Ildikó was also an active participant in the events, together with her husband. Those were busy days.

After about ten days the revolution's first phase ended in jubilation. The Russians withdrew their forces from Budapest and allowed the formation of a Hungarian government with Imre Nagy as the prime minister. It seemed that the revolutionaries—fighters and demonstrators—having the truth and right on their side, defeated the wild beast.

The fighting over, I joined the large number of inhabitants of the city who poured onto the streets in the area where most of the fighting occurred. Viewing the damage caused by and to the Russian forces, I realized the real extent of ruin. Many buildings were destroyed, and disabled Soviet military equipment and dead bodies covered the streets.

Although ecstatic, I felt extremely guilty. Walking along the streets of the *free* city of Budapest, seeing the signs of revolution everywhere, I was immersed in my thoughts: "How could I have doubted our victory? The unselfish sacrifice of all those dead and wounded revolutionary heroes?" Seeing the makeshift burial grounds in the war-torn streets, I blamed myself. "Should I and could I have done more if I had had the real conviction in winning against the might of the Soviet Union?"

Mother was happy and sad at the same time. "It's a great pity," she said, "that your father did not live to see the end of communism."

I also felt unhappy that my father could not enjoy the communists' humiliation.

We celebrated the revolution's victory too soon. Later events bore out my earlier suspicions. The Russians, we found out, were only biding their time. Realizing that their invading armed forces became influenced by the revolution, the Russians withdrew them. They brought in fresh replacements directly from the Soviet Union and stationed them just outside Budapest. Prime Minister Nagy requested a conversation with the Soviet ambassador, Yuri Andropov, and questioned him about the intentions of the occupying forces. Andropov, who later became the Soviet dictator, assured Nagy that the troops would be withdrawn.

Disregarding accepted international rules of war, the Russians devised a plan of deceit. Under the leadership of General Malinin, the Soviets started discussions in the Parliament building regarding the withdrawal of their troops from Hungary. We heard about this news with great satisfaction. Soon, we believed, there would be no need for the signs one could see all over the city: "Russki, go home!"

Under the pretext of continuing the negotiations, on November 3 the Russian generals lured the Hungarian military leaders to their camp outside the city limits. There Serov, head of the Soviet secret police, appeared and ordered the arrest of the Hungarian military leaders. The Soviet troops attacked early the following day.

During this second Soviet invasion, there were no doubts about the Russian troops' behavior. On Sunday morning, November 4, 1956, my family and the entire city woke up to the noises of invasion: Russian tanks rolling on every major artery of Budapest's inner area. The soldiers manning these tanks were not confused, although they could not know what was really happening in Hungary. Their orders were clear: keep on shooting at anything and anybody, terrorizing the city's population.

József Boulevard became a war zone again. When Mother, Grandmother, Ildikó, her husband, and I were awakened early Sunday morning by the explosions, we quickly jumped out of bed. It did not take long before the tragic facts became apparent: the country's short-lived freedom was being crushed. This was the third time during the revolution that I felt let down. At the start of the revolution I feared that great danger might result from the outburst of unchecked emotions. During the time of short freedom I blamed myself for not believing in victory. Now the realization came that all was lost. Still, I had to make sure that it was indeed a Russian invasion.

There were no Russian tanks immediately in front of our building, so I opened a window and leaned out to confirm what I already knew. That move was a big mistake.

"Run, quickly!" I yelled to the other members of my family. "A tank is approaching. They may have seen me."

We assembled in the little room facing the interior courtyard. The five of us felt a little safer there, away from the József Boulevard frontage.

The barrage now sounded from a close distance. "It would be safer in the shelter," suggested Mother. In that instant, a tremendous explosion almost split our eardrums. Aunt Lili, had she been there, would have yelled: "This is the end!" This time it almost was, for my entire family.

"They did see you!" screamed Ildikó.

A tank bullet flew into our apartment through a window, pierced through two brick walls, exited into the main staircase and reentered the L-shaped apartment at its vestibule, where it exploded. Mother did not have to repeat her suggestion about going to the shelter.

Rushing to the basement, we noticed that people were racing to the same part of the shelter they had occupied during the war, about a decade before. New tenants were less familiar with the surroundings and took more time to settle. Among them was the wife of the only communist in our building. Realizing the extent of destruction that was taking place throughout the city and noticing the tenants' reactions, she looked around nervously.

"This is terrible," she volunteered grudgingly. "They shouldn't just shoot indiscriminately at anything."

Nobody was impressed by her admission. As always, we ignored her. The only reactions she received from us were dirty looks of contempt.

A few careless people evidently could not believe the extent of the invading troops' cruelty, their determination to shoot at anything and anybody. A stranger lay dead in front of our apartment building with a loaf of bread under his arm. I had seen many people killed during the war and revolution, but for me the picture of this man, clutching the loaf of bread even in his death, epitomized the wanton destruction of human life. The poor victim's body was there all day; it could be moved from the sidewalk only under cover of darkness. The Russian tanks stopped shooting continuously, but they fired at anybody appearing on the streets or looking out windows.

Nineteen fifty–six was a presidential election year in the United States, with the actual balloting only two days after the second Soviet invasion. The word spread among those who still believed in victory that President Dwight Eisenhower would not interfere before the election but might provide help after the following Tuesday. Radio Free Europe and Voice of America broadcast the events of the revolution. Listening to the glowing accounts, many believed that the West would interfere and help Hungary to obtain its freedom.

"Hold on for at least two days, till the American elections," advised the fighters who took up their weapons again.

But the West did not interfere. The United States, main adversary of Soviet imperialism, was unprepared for the events that took place in Hungary. In June, 1956, the National Security Council expressed the opinion that a revolution in Hungary was not possible. When facts contradicted this assumption, President Eisenhower ordered a new, and belated, study of possible strategies concerning the communist satellites in Europe.

The Russians misled the United States as well about the Soviet troops' intentions in Hungary. Charles Bohlen, the American ambassador in Moscow, reported that Marshall Zukov, the Soviet minister of defense, ordered the withdrawal of his forces from Budapest.

Diplomatic communication between the United States and Hungary was difficult during the revolution. A new ambassador, Edward Wailes, arrived in Budapest at the end of October, at the height of the turmoil. He had little knowledge of Hungary and was instructed not to make contact with Nagy's government. Being a former communist, Nagy did not enjoy the full trust of Washington.

Since many in Hungary continued to believe that support would soon arrive from the West, the fighting continued.

During the evening of the second Soviet invasion, when the Russian tanks disappeared from our street and found safer surroundings, I hurried out to help build barricades to hamper the tanks' movements. My participation in this activity was fueled by a sense of duty rather then the conviction that there was still hope.

Some of the fighters dismantled the streetcars' heavy overhead wires and laid them across the roadway. They knew that one way of rendering the tanks motionless was to entangle the wires in their caterpillar treads.

While building a barricade, I noticed that one of the men who was working in my group seemed familiar. I recognized that I had seen him at a newly formed democratic party's meeting. "So, the opposition party is represented on the barricades," I remarked to him.

He did not recognize me. "How do you know about my involvement in the party?" His face showed grave concern.

"I was there too. But don't worry. Not as a communist spy."

"It doesn't matter. They'll find out anyway, if we lose. In that case I've had it." He shrugged, and we continued to loosen the roadway's cobblestones with our makeshift tools.

The next day the fighting again intensified in our area. Piled a few feet high, the cobblestones and other barricades slowed down the tanks' movements, but the Soviet military might could not be stopped without outside help. Riding in with the Soviet tanks, the communist leaders quickly formed a new government and took over the radio station. I listened with horror to a broadcast that revealed the communists' determination to regain control. The announcement quoted a well-known poem containing a reference to the fact that under certain circumstances entire nations can disappear from the face of the earth:

• • •

Nations surround the grave
where a country lies,
Millions cry and mourn
with painful sighs.

This was a powerful and frightening message, threatening the entire nation with the highest degree of ethnic cleansing, genocide. I knew that the communists could go to extremes, but threatening the entire nation with extinction?

"The bastards!" I burst out, as tears swelled in my eyes.

"What is it?" asked my mother, who wasn't listening to the broadcast.

"Nothing can help us now, Mother. Nothing."

Realizing the dangerous situation and the hopelessness of the revolution without the help of the United States, some of the Western relief agencies and correspondents covering the events began to leave the country.

Géza Madarász, a friend of mine who joined the revolution from a labor camp, was filmed by a crew from the well-known American television network NBC. He also interpreted for the NBC staff. After the second, fierce Russian invasion, representatives of the network decided to leave the country while they still could. Saying good-bye to Géza, the leader of the group thanked him for his help. "If you ever come to New York, look me up," he said in a casual manner.

Only a few weeks later, Géza surprised the man in New York. Géza got a job and worked at NBC until his retirement.

The exodus began.

Laci Huszár, with whom I spent much time in the shelter during the last days of World War II, decided to leave a few weeks after the second Russian invasion. He is now an architect in London, England. "But I want to do something, to help the country," he said to me before leaving, as we discussed the hopeless situation.

When he arrived in Vienna, Laci, as a representative of the Hungarian University Students' Revolutionary Committee, wrote an open letter to India's Prime Minister Jawaharlal Nehru, self-appointed leader of the nonaligned nations. Outside the communist camp, Nehru was one of the few leaders, who, for political reasons, did not openly condemn the Soviet Union for its invasion of Hungary. I heard Laci's open letter read in Radio Free Europe, urging Nehru to take a moral stand.

Laci handed his letter personally to the Indian representative Sir V. C. Raghavan. In it he wrote: "When a foreign power invaded our country, the Hungarian people expected India's diplomatic support. Your lack of action deeply disappointed our nation. . . . We respectfully request Prime Minister Nehru to send his personal representative to Hungary without delay, to start negotiations between the Soviet and Hungarian governments, supporting our interests for freedom and independence."

Help had not come from the West, at least not to free Hungary from the grips of the Soviet Union. Imre Nagy and members of his cabinet fled to the Yugoslav embassy. The Russians crowned their series of dishonorable acts. Their tanks fired into the Yugoslav embassy, killing a diplomat. Later they abducted Nagy and his companions, after luring them out of the embassy by promising them safe conduct. Not willing to renounce the revolution, Nagy was later sentenced to death and executed during the period of terror that followed the uprising.

At that time it seemed that the Hungarian Revolution of 1956 ended in total defeat for the freedom fighters. In retrospect it is clear that the revolution achieved immense results. It broke the power of the strong Western European communist parties, notably in Italy and France, where disillusioned leftists stopped supporting Soviet communism. The revolution also paved the way to a communist system in Hungary that later provided a better way of life and more freedom than in other countries in the Soviet camp. To avoid another confrontation, Soviet leaders did not force a Stalinist government on Hungary again. Slowly, the country, partly because of contacts with former refugees settling in capitalist countries, shifted closer and closer to the West. Finally the reformed communist leaders decided to yield power to a freely elected government.

Eventually, the Hungarians were also able to cause the overthrow of communism in East Germany and Czechoslovakia. In 1989, the Hungarian rulers, officially still communists, defied the Soviet Union and allowed visitors from other Warsaw Pact countries to leave for the West through the Hungarian border. Because of that action, the conservative communist governments of East Germany and Czechoslovakia lost control over their populations, who then demanded and achieved democratic elections.

It is easy now, decades later, to think of the Hungarian Revolution's results with satisfaction. Then, in November, 1956, my fellow Hungarians and I felt differently. Helplessness, hatred, fear, and mistrust in the future overshadowed our lives. These feelings drove many of us to leave our country of birth, away from the grips of a communist dictatorship that was ready to unleash its vengeance after the fall of the revolution.

My sons, Gordon and Nicholas.

The Coronation Church in Budapest. Courtesy Norbert Wissnyi.

My parents' wedding photo.

My newly wed parents return to their home in Ujszász.

Ildikó put me in the dog house.

With Ildikó in our courtyard in Ujszász, where the little gypsy girl used to sing.

József Boulevard now, from our old apartment window.

Ildikó at seventeen, around the time of the siege of Budapest.

Dr. Huszár, fall of 1943, on József Blvd. Courtesy Laszlo Huszár.

Dr. Huszár and his son Laci with his friend Zsolt in 1942. Courtesy Laszlo Huszár.

A residential area of Budapest after the siege. Courtesy MTI Hungarian News Agency.

Much of Budapest lay in ruin. Courtesy MTI Hungarian News Agency.

Margaret Bridge is replaced by the first temporary bridge, nicknamed Margie. Courtesy MTI Hungarian News Agency.

The rush to the countryside in search of food. Courtesy MTI Hungarian News Agency.

At the Budapest junior tennis championships in 1948. I was on the winning Teglas-Palotas team, at right.

The Technical University of Budapest. Courtesy Norbert Wissnyi.

My friend Attila, who survived three days of torture.

The demonstrators confused the Russian invaders. Courtesy MTI Hungarian News Agency.

The short side street where the projectile from a Russian tank's cannon almost killed me.

Curious onlookers view the damage caused to and by the Russian forces. Courtesy Laszlo Papp.

Disabled Russian military equipment and dead bodies covered the streets. Courtesy Laszlo Papp.

Damage caused by now-disabled Russian military equipment. Courtesy Laszlo Papp.

Makeshift burials on the war-torn streets. Courtesy Laszlo Papp.

Csaba Teglas and Rudi Kriegler at the time of our escape.

*My favorite sculpture.
Courtesy Norbert
Wissnyi.*

*My mother, who was greatly sad-
dened by my departure.*

*Grandmother on her 100th birthday.
Courtesy Csaba Szabo.*

Studying in the apartment I shared with Rudi in Toronto.

Mother with her brothers, Karl and Julius. Courtesy Csaba Szabo.

The storytellers: Aunts Zelma, Gizi, and Ella.

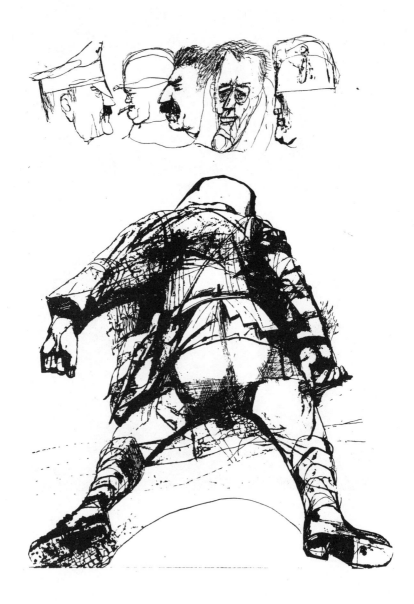

9

THROUGH THE
IRON CURTAIN

"Dad, tell us about the gun again," said Gordon. "And your escape from Hungary."

I was startled. My boys forgot most of the details of my escape through the Iron Curtain, but the story of the revolver fascinated them, although that weapon had very little to do with my travel to freedom.

It was November 22, 1956, nearly a month after the outbreak of the revolution against the communist regime. My friend Rudi Kriegler called. Surprisingly, throughout the revolution with all the fighting going on, the telephones worked.

"What do you think?" Rudi asked, continuing a discussion we had the previous day. "Maybe it's time to leave."

I looked at my mother, who was listening to my conversation. Would it break her heart? I agreed with my friend. "I think we'd better. It's getting tougher and tougher every day. What about tomorrow morning?"

The sounds of guns had been replaced by screams of the wounded, and cries of relatives and friends of the dead. While the government-controlled radio was broadcasting empty promises of amnesty for all those who stopped fighting or demonstrating and returned to work, arrests and deportations began. The Soviet troops and their puppet Hungarian government were almost in total control. It was time for all to realize that the West would not come to the aid of the Hungarian freedom fighters who so gallantly took on the communist oppressors and their Soviet supporters.

Life suddenly seemed hopeless and frightening. Rudi and I were in our mid-twenties, well-educated, full of energy, but without much of a future after the recent events. I had met Rudi and a number of other physicists through playing bridge, which was allowed in Hungary, even on an organized level. Other communist countries, notably Romania, prohibited any kind of card playing even as late as the 1980s. People of that country assigned the values of cards to domino pieces and pretended to play that game to avoid persecution. Hungarian communist rulers, especially after Stalin's death, demonstrated moderation in this respect. After all, Hungary was always closer to the West not only geographically but in spirit as well. Total elimination of the Western way of life would have been difficult.

Rudi and I decided that, like many others, we would not want to live through a communist takeover a second time. To live under communism is bad enough; far worse is the period when the dictatorship takes control by eliminating all opposition. Unfortunately, our fears later proved justified. Many friends and relatives who stayed home suffered severe hardships after the revolution. My Uncle Karl was punished with a jail term for his participation in the uprising. It was no consolation for him at that time that in the 1990s a stadium would be named after him in the city where he was a gym teacher and respected basketball coach. My sister was dismissed from her job and she and her husband, both professionals, had to perform hard physical labor for a number of years. Ildikó was forced to continue that kind of work even while pregnant with her first child. Labor laws to protect the unborn meant nothing in those days.

Within a few months, 200,000 people, mostly young and skilled, left the country of ten million to avoid persecution and find a better way of life. Rudi and I had more than one reason to leave. We wanted to avoid a jail sentence or deportation to a Siberian gulag, and the possibility of living in a democratic and prosperous country also influenced us. Although the arguments were overwhelmingly in favor of our escaping the communist oppression, the decision to leave our country, families, and friends was made with great reluctance.

After my telephone conversation with Rudi I looked at my mother. I still remember the sad expression on her face as she asked me.

"Are you leaving?"

I nodded. "Only for a few years. Things will have to change soon."

I did not really believe that communism would collapse within the foreseeable future, but I hoped that it would substantially change soon and I could come home.

My mother just looked at me. Now that I have children of my own, I understand better how difficult it must have been for her to accept my decision to leave the country. My thoughts centered more on my desire to avoid the communists' repercussions than on my departure's long-term effect on my family.

I found my knapsack and started packing. There was room only for a change of underwear, a few sandwiches, and a number of technical books. I could not resist putting a couple of my favorite novels in the knapsack as well. Even for one who loves literature as much as I do, this act seemed rather inappropriate, to say the least. To escape through the Iron Curtain and rescue a few novels! At least I was reasonable in selecting my clothes. I put on sturdy boots and pants in anticipation of the long walk we would have to take at the border. I also took the small amount of savings I had in a paper box in a cupboard.

Our apartment, centrally located and along the main thoroughfare of József Boulevard in Pest, was the place where we usually gathered before our youthful activities. This time was no exception; Rudi came by a few hours after our conversation.

After discussing our plans and saying short but painful good-byes, near sundown we started walking toward the railway station in Buda, from where the trains left to the West. Stepping outside the gate of our apartment building I missed the familiar sights and sounds of the city. No street-cars or buses were running, and the signs of fighting were all around us: burnt out Russian tanks, barricades, war-torn buildings, and makeshift graves in the small parks. Although organized armed resistance practically ceased, the country was still in a turmoil with strikes, sporadic skirmishes, and demonstrations.

At the first intersection, where signs of the fierce fighting of a few days ago could be seen on the buildings, my favorite sculpture stood unharmed. A little boy crying—a dog is tearing his clothes while he tries to hold onto a stolen rooster. The boy's crying seemed more appropriate than usual. Farther on, the effects of the recent fighting had not changed Calvin Square. It had not been fixed up yet from the destruction of World War II.

Crossing over the Danube to Buda, we viewed the beautiful bridges that, with the exception of one, had been rebuilt since the war. I looked toward Margaret Bridge where my Aunt Piri stood for hours in a street-car in 1944, in water up to her waist. The city at that time was still controlled by the retreating Nazis. A few spans of Margaret Bridge, mined by the Nazis, blew up by accident well before it was supposed to, and Aunt Piri had stories to tell for years to come. Fortunately, no harm came to the bridges this time.

In Buda, we passed my alma mater, the Technical University of Budapest, and soon reached our preliminary destination, the apartment of a friend who lived near the station. Rudi and I planned to sleep there in order to get a head start in the morning and catch the first available train, if one would be running at all.

We could not sleep much. Steve, a few years our junior and an only child, decided to join us, against the wishes of his widowed mother. Lying in makeshift beds, we listened all night to her heartbreaking cries and sobs from the adjoining room. Greatly saddened by this display of love and despair I thought of my own mother who might have been in a similar state of mind.

In the morning, Steve's mother begged him, still sobbing, to stay home, whatever the consequences. Finally, to our relief, he relented.

"Let's leave quickly," said Rudi, "before Steve changes his mind again."

"Good idea," I responded. "I wouldn't want to be responsible for breaking his mother's heart."

I learned years later that a few days after our stay at their apartment, Steve had to leave anyway. Suspicious characters were inquiring in the neighborhood about his activities during the revolution, and he found it advisable to find his way to Austria.

We hurried to the railroad station in the hope of catching a train that would take us close enough to the Austrian border. On the north, east, and south, Hungary was surrounded by communist countries. Austria was the only democracy along our borders. To the south, Marshal Tito's communist Yugoslavia was not in the Russian camp and offered a possible but questionable choice. It was not known at that time whether refugees fleeing to Yugoslavia would be forcibly returned to Hungary or not. We had no specific plans yet. We just wanted to get near the Austrian border, and then we knew we would have to feel our way.

By the time Rudi and I arrived at the railway station, the large waiting hall was filled with people, most of them dressed in conspicuously "rugged" attire. Wearing our boots, pullovers, light overcoats, and knapsacks we blended in with the crowd. We could hardly be mistaken for business travelers.

"Looks like most people here have the same idea as we do," I said.

Nevertheless, at first Rudi and I discussed our plans only in whispers. In a little while familiar faces appeared here and there, and these acquaintances confirmed our suspicion that their destination was the same as ours. It did not take too long before almost the entire waiting crowd was openly discussing the possibilities and chances of escaping through the dreaded Iron Curtain.

After a long wait, finally a train pulled in—but already filled to the point that only a few additional people were able to board it. We were lucky for not being able to leave with that train; we found out later that it was thoroughly checked by the much-feared secret police and the Russians at the next stop. Many of the passengers were arrested or sent back to Budapest.

The next train left in a couple of hours and took us without any problem to the city of Győr, about thirty miles from the Austrian border. To our great surprise, in this city of about eighty thousand the revolution had not died yet. Local newspapers were still printing anticommunist articles, and there were no Russian soldiers in sight. The communists simply ignored Győr and concentrated on the capital. After all, they reasoned, events taking place in Budapest determined the future of the entire country.

At the station and in the square in front of it, people openly engaged in discussions about the best way to approach the heavily guarded border. Some groups decided on walking; others chose the bus or train to reach the proximity of the Iron Curtain. A few optimists rented taxis and wanted to arrive in Vienna in style, reasoning that there are no land mines and barbed wire fences at the official crossings. They hoped to bluff or bribe their way to Austria in the general turmoil. I know now that many thousands were caught, shot, or turned back at the border. I always wondered how many, if any, made it in this elegant way, in a taxi.

Milling around Station Square discussing the possibilities of escape, we met a business acquaintance with the same first name as mine. Joining forces with Csaba Szilágyi, a mining engineer, from that moment on we formed a threesome that remained inseparable until we reached our final destination overseas.

We appreciated Csaba's company not only because he became a good friend but also because he spoke fluent Russian. Csaba was the son of a poor factory worker with many children. After graduating from high school he welcomed a scholarship to a Moscow university in the workers' paradise. The drawback of his free education was that during the summer holidays at home he could not walk the streets safely after dark. His neighbors took him for a Muscovite (a person who served the interests of the Russian communists) and beat him up a couple of times. Having had enough of this treatment, Csaba transferred to a Hungarian university for the last two years of his studies and slowly regained the acceptance of his childhood friends.

After long deliberation, we decided to get closer to the border by train. The distance to Austria was far too great to walk, and the buses too confining in case of an inspection. However, we elected not to take the shortest route most people chose. It seemed far safer to travel toward Sopron, in a longer but less conspicuous direction. That decision proved to be wise. On the train the majority of people were bona fide travelers, many of them commuters going home to the villages from Győr. But there were also quite a few heading for Austria.

To increase our chances of escape, the three of us conducted a survey among the inhabitants of the border villages traveling on the train. We wanted to know whether there were only Russian soldiers patrolling in their villages or Hungarian guards too. Our intention was to cross the Iron Curtain at a location with few Russian soldiers, whom we believed to be far more trigger-happy than the Hungarian patrols. The Hungarian guards were not enthusiastic about shooting their fellow citizens.

At the proper time the conductor announced throughout the train: "Next station is the last one with few Russian patrols. All those heading toward Austria may wish to disembark and continue on foot." His open behavior was another sign that, like in Győr, regardless of the loss of the revolution, the Muscovites had not had a chance yet to consolidate their power.

It was dark, around five in the evening, when, in addition to the local inhabitants, about twenty of us would-be refugees (all young men and women) got off the train at Fertőd. Some of those wishing to go to Austria continued on to Sopron, the place closest to the border.

Fertőd, a small village, is about a half a mile from the railroad station. When the locals started walking toward the village, we joined them, forming one group, hoping that inquisitive eyes would take us for commuters going home after a day's work. Realizing right away what was happening, the locals cooperated, and the two groups of people were well mixed together.

Our precaution saved us: about halfway to the village an armed patrol passed by but in the dark did not notice anything suspicious and allowed our group to proceed.

The border is on the far side of the village, about seven or eight miles away. We hoped to obtain valuable information from the locals that would help us to pick the right place for crossing. As a result of quiet probing, a young man about twenty-five whispered into my ear. "Just follow me. I live at the end of the village, the last house."

Rudi and I motioned to the others, and at our preliminary destination the entire group entered the young man's yard, on which stood a house typical of Hungarian peasant villages. The long, narrow, one-story structure lay perpendicular to the street so that its yard lay not at the back but at the side of the property. The porch, along the full length of the house, served purposes related to agricultural work such as husking corn. A dim light filtered through the kitchen window. A solid wood fence enclosed the yard; in the dark nobody could see us from the street. The young man was very nervous, realizing the danger to himself. His helping our escape could be discovered by the communists. Still, he agreed to walk with our group to a certain point near the border and provide much-needed information.

Through the fields, from the back of his house, the young man led the way. Walking along the furrows required some effort; the earth was wet and stuck to our boots. Meanwhile our guide wanted to hear about the events in the capital and asked many questions.

"Is it true that the Russians destroyed a large part of the city? Are they arresting many people? Do the workers still demonstrate and strike?"

Rudi and I tried to answer the guide's questions, but we cut the responses short; our thoughts were on our impending escape. The young man, sensing our tenseness, stopped asking questions.

After walking a few miles, we arrived at the end of the cultivated fields, reaching the restricted area that even the local inhabitants were prohibited to enter. Our guide stopped. "This is as far as I can take you." He started to describe the locations of Russian and Hungarian guardhouses and the natural and manmade obstacles. Trying in the dark to visualize the area as the young man described it, we hoped that his information was sufficient to help us find our way.

"What about minefields?" asked Csaba.

"I don't know anything about land mines. Anyway, if you follow the route I described you should be all right. I see the border guards walking in that direction to their huts all the time." Wishing us good luck, he, our last human contact with anyone in our country, disappeared in the dark. There was not enough time to express our gratitude to him properly before he departed. For a few minutes I looked after the disappearing figure in no man's land. I felt concern, doubt, and sadness. Later I often wondered whether our guide had to pay dearly for his kindness once the communists tightened their grip again on every aspect of life in the entire country.

But this was not the time and location for reflection. Lightning rockets illuminating the sky, and sporadic gunfire forced us to concentrate on the next move. How many of the bullets were actually directed at people and how many were just fired in the air to scare refugees away from the border we did not know, and were not keen to find out.

By this time Rudi, Csaba, and I emerged as the leaders of the group. I stopped those who started walking in the general direction of the border. "Wait a minute. Let's think a little about what we'll have to do," I said.

"First of all, does anyone have a gun or other weapon?" Rudi asked.

One fellow, George, proudly displayed his handgun. This is the gun my children remembered so well.

"Get rid of that weapon please," I said, "or we'll have to take different routes."

"We may need a gun," George tried to insist, but I pointed in the direction of the heavy gunfire.

"You want to fight the Russian army with one pistol? That gun can only get us into trouble. If we make it, it will not be by force. What we need is good planning, and some luck."

After a short discussion, the majority of the group agreed with Rudi and me and demanded that George get rid of his gun. We were all pleased when we saw him unload the gun and throw it away.

"The three of us," offered Csaba, as he pointed at Rudi and me, "will go ahead, look at the terrain, and try to find a good crossing point. The entire group walking together or wandering around could be detected much easier than the three of us. I speak Russian, so I'll lead the way in case we run into Ivan. I might be able to hear what they're talking about, and if they find us, I might be able to talk our way out of trouble."

Rudi and I were to keep contact with the group. Everybody realized quickly that Csaba's suggestion made good sense, and no one disagreed with the plan.

To scout the area took some time. It was difficult to see in the dark, and whenever the flares lit up the sky we had to duck and take cover to avoid detection. We also had to make sure not to stray from the area our guide described, to protect ourselves from land mines. Fortunately, our guide had given good directions, and after a while a possible crossing point appeared a few hundred yards from the bushes that gave us cover. The small abandoned railroad bridge, spanning a narrow waterway that may have been a canal or creek, looked promising. It seemed highly unlikely that the bridge would be mined, but a large patrol booth nearby presented a possible danger. Staying low, we tried to figure out whether the guards were Russians or Hungarians, how good their line of vision was towards the bridge, and what their schedule of patrolling might be.

"I think this location will be all right," said Rudi. "A quick run from this position should give us a good chance when the guards are in the booth, not out on patrol near the bridge."

"Yes, I think so," I agreed, "if we run fast in the dark and immediately after the launching of a flare, when the guards may be blinded for a few seconds."

Rudi concurred. "Let's get the others. Those uniforms looked Hungarian. Even if they see us they may not shoot without warning. I don't think we'll find a better place to cross."

As Rudi and I crept back to the group, Mary, a girl of about eighteen exclaimed: "I told you they'd be back!"

It dawned on me that, indeed, the three of us could have gone over the border by ourselves much easier than with the entire group. Of course, such treachery had not even crossed our minds.

"There's a crossing place nearby that seems pretty safe," I said. "However, the guards may be on the alert. In that case, our only hope is that they will not shoot first and ask questions later."

"Or that their aim is not very good in the dark," added Rudi. "But remember, once we start moving near the border you may not be able to turn back without risking your own life as well as everybody else's."

The long silence indicated the determination of our companions. It seemed that nobody, coming this far, wanted to turn back.

I started walking. "Let's not waste time. Csaba is waiting for us."

Rudi and I led the group toward the border, covering ourselves from the direction of the patrol booth, showing more confidence in our sense of direction than was warranted. We found Csaba with surprising ease, at the prearranged location, observing the guards. Heavy gunfire sounded in the distance, but fortunately it was quiet nearby.

After assembling behind bushes, we began discussing how to make our dash when suddenly flares lit the sky, and a couple of border guards stepped outside of their booths.

"Down!" whispered a number of us, and we hugged the ground.

"If you guys hadn't made me throw away my gun," said George, "I could get closer and shoot them."

"Sure," I said, "and then you'd shoot an entire army that would come after us."

Whether or not the guards saw or heard any of us I do not know, but they blindly shot a few bursts out of their submachine guns.

A young woman I will call Cathy suddenly started shaking with fright. "I can't do it," she said. "Leave me here."

"That would be dangerous," I said. "After we make a run for the border, the guards will search the area and find you."

"You'll just have to come with us," insisted George.

"George, we can't force anybody," said Rudi. "Who knows what will happen to us. Nobody can take the responsibility for someone else."

"Damn it," responded George angrily, "I am not going to turn back and rot in a communist jail or in a Russian gulag just because this chick lost her nerve!"

Csaba approached Cathy. "You'll have to make up your mind. Either go back right now on your own or come with us. If you turn back, we'll give you ten minutes to get out of this dangerous area."

After some thought, Cathy pulled herself together. "All right, I'll come with you. I have to. My husband fought against the Russians before he was killed, and the secret police were looking for me."

Finally, we could discuss how to get across the border. First, all of us would creep as close to the bridge as possible, under cover of the sparse vegetation. Then, first Rudi, who spoke German well, was to rush forward with the girls from the edge of the clearing. The five or six girls would obviously run slower than the young men, but we did not want them to be left behind. A few seconds later I was to follow with the rest of the group, and Csaba was to be the last, in case his Russian would be needed.

I had an additional suggestion. "George, would you be willing to go with the first group and help Cathy in case she has difficulties?"

"What do you want me to do with her if she acts up?" asked George, somewhat annoyed. "Spank her, strangle her, or carry her on my shoulder?"

"George, you look like the strongest fellow among us," said Rudi. "I am sure you could carry Cathy a few yards if you had to."

"Sure, sure," said George, still annoyed but appreciating the comment about his physical powers. He turned to Cathy. "All right, baby, we'll travel together."

Approaching the bridge was not as easy as it seemed. In November, without leaves on the trees, the vegetation did not provide much cover. We had to crawl in the dirt and mud. Occasionally I glanced at Cathy with concern. Surprisingly, she seemed to appreciate George's help, and George obviously was enjoying his role as her "guardian."

"Come on, baby, or we'll still be here at daybreak," he whispered to her when she started lagging behind.

Near the bridge the ground was cleared of all vegetation to allow the guards to see any possible movement. We looked at each other. "This is it," I thought, and I am sure everyone else felt the moment's importance. There was no need for any more discussion. We understood each other.

A last glance around to make sure that all of us were ready, and Rudi motioned to the girls. They stood up at the same time and started running. The rest of us followed immediately.

Ta-ta-ta-ta-ta . . . Boom! Submachine guns started chattering as the first few reached the bridge, and the sky turned orange and red. Still, nobody wavered; we ran and ran as fast as we could. I caught up with the girls and saw George pulling Cathy by the hand. There was no more reason to whisper; he yelled encouragingly and as loudly as he could. "Let's go, baby, just one more minute and we're free!"

We all reached the far side of the waterway, exhausted, and a few collapsed. Csaba, the last man, dashed over the bridge and into the safety of woods. "Are we in Austria?" he asked excitedly.

"We made it, we made it!" someone exclaimed. "We all made it!"

"We sure did," yelled George and gave a friendly kiss to Cathy.

Just as we collected ourselves and started thinking about what direction to take, a calm man representing the well-known relief organization appeared with a huge red cross covering his chest and smiled.

"Welcome to the West. Is everybody all right?" After being assured that none of us received any injuries, he continued. "All right then, let's go into the Austrian village of Pamhagen."

During those troubled times the border guards were overworked. They—especially the Hungarian ones, under the influence of the revolution—were also less than enthusiastic about their dirty work. Were they really aiming at us with their submachine guns, or only trying to frighten our group away from the border? Did our well-chosen position restrict their shooting, lest the bullets invade Austrian territory? Whether the guards helped us or our success was owing entirely to good preparation I do not know. At any rate, unlike many others who banded together to increase their chances for a successful crossing, all members of our group escaped without a mishap.

Before we started walking toward the Austrian village, Rudi and I stopped for a few seconds, looking back in the direction of the border. I looked at my watch. "It's midnight," I said quietly. "Beginning of a new day." Rudi just nodded.

We turned around and began walking toward an unknown new life.

Although elated about our recently acquired freedom, the tragic events of the recent past weighed heavily upon us. The full realization that we were free at last, no longer puppets whose strings were held by the communists, came later.

10

NO OCEAN LINER

"Dad, wouldn't you like to take a cruise once?" asked Gordon. "Older people like those kinds of vacations."

So I graduated to that age group. An older man. "No, Gordon, I am not particularly interested in a cruise. Once I had the opportunity to travel on an ocean liner free of charge, but I had to decline the offer."

"Why did you do that? And when did it happen?"

"That was a long time ago, after I escaped from Hungary."

From the Hungarian border, the Red Cross representative led our group of refugees into the village of Pamhagen, where a large number of compatriots had already been provided with transient quarters in a school building. After we spent the night on improvised sleeping cots, a train took all the fugitives from Pamhagen to the largest refugee camp near Vienna, in the city of Traiskirchen.

About five thousand people found temporary homes in the former military barracks that were built for the Hapsburg Army. During World War II, Nazi soldiers were stationed there, and later Russian forces occupied the buildings until 1954, when they withdrew from the country. It was that withdrawal that made our escape possible. Had the Soviet army still been in the eastern part of Austria during the Hungarian Revolution, its troops would have prevented us from crossing the border.

Most of the refugees in Traiskirchen were young single men, but a few women and families provided welcome variety. The straw mattresses were comfortable enough, and the food included such delicacies as oranges and lemons, fruits we had not seen in Hungary for years. By the time of our arrival many countries had offices and representatives within the walled-in compound, recruiting actively the young able-bodied and skilled people but offering refuge to all. While they hadn't helped Hungary to gain its freedom, all the Western countries felt obligated at least to take care of those who fled the communist oppression. Immigration requests received approval within days or weeks, and transportation to their final destinations was arranged for the refugees free of charge.

Rudi, Csaba, and I were not yet ready to make a decision about which country we would settle in. In the faint hope that the situation in Hungary might still change for the better, we were biding our time. We also wanted to gather information on the recruiting countries and if possible agree on the same destination.

The banks provided no exchange for currencies of communist countries. An enterprising man who arrived in the camp well before us established contact with black marketers for the purpose of exchanging Hungarian currency for Austrian. Because of the uncertain situation in Hungary, the exchange rate was about half of what it should have been. Nevertheless, the black market rate was better than having no shillings at all.

Having acquired sufficient Austrian money for the commuter train ride, Rudi and I decided to visit Vienna. I was anxious to get to the capital to pick up my mail at the main post office. Before leaving home, I asked my mother to write to me there, poste restante.

Access into and out of the camp was controlled and limited. Permission was required for our trip to Vienna. Waiting for our turn to see the person in charge, we sat patiently in the crowded vestibule of the camp's office when an Austrian woman and her young daughter appeared. We quickly offered our seats to them.

"Danke schön," said the woman. She listened to her daughter, who whispered something in her ear. The woman nodded as they were ushered into the office out of turn.

When the woman and her daughter were leaving, the officer called Rudi and me. After giving us passes to Vienna, he conveyed a surprising invitation.

"Mrs. Pandak, the lady who was just here with her daughter Suzy, would like to invite you two for dinner on Sunday. Would you like to go? They live near, in the city of Baden."

Of course, we happily accepted.

"Mrs. Pandak came to the office to invite a couple of refugees of my choosing," continued the officer, "but meeting you she decided to ask for your company specifically." He handed us the Pandaks' address and another pass for Sunday.

The family dinner was a pleasant change from the company of thousands of refugees and lineups at meal time. Although my German was rather rusty, I was able to make elementary conversation. That Sunday dinner was the best reward I have ever received for a simple polite gesture. I exchanged letters with Suzy for a long time and spent a wonderful week with her years later, on my first trip back to Europe.

Invitation to the Pandaks was only one of the expressions of sympathy we enjoyed in Austria. News describing the terrible conditions in Hungary saddened not only us but the Austrians as well. Since part of that country was occupied by the Russians after the war until 1954, the Austrian people had a special appreciation of our situation. The effusion of kindness toward refugees was apparent everywhere, with people trying to help at every opportunity. Even beggars offered to share the alms they received with refugees. On the commuter train to Vienna, a man offered me a roll of banknotes, which I politely refused.

In Vienna, I was happy to learn that a letter was waiting for me at the post office. The communists were trying to prove to the world that order in Hungary was being restored. They were eager to normalize the mail service, but because of censorship my mother's letter did not include controversial political subjects. Mother expressed hope that I was all right and begged me to write as soon as possible. I immediately responded, assuring her that Rudi and I were well and promising to write regularly.

On the way back to Traiskirchen, I again met with the kindness of the Austrian people. Unfortunately, on that occasion I was not allowed to reject help.

Waiting for the train on that cold day, I inquired about the price of a cup of tea at the station's restaurant. Realizing that I could afford that luxury, I sat down in the warm establishment. A man sitting at the next table had ordered a snack but, seeing that my tight budget allowed me to have only a cup of tea, asked the waiter to serve me his plate of food. My protests were to no avail, the waiter put the plate of herrings in front of me with such determination that I had to understand: he and the customer would not take no for an answer.

I realize that being shot at by a Russian tank, living through a revolution, and escaping through the Iron Curtain are terrible experiences. Still, in my memory that plate of herrings is just as frightening. I absolutely *hate* herrings. They revolt me, but what could I do? As a poor refugee, cold and hungry, could I tell my benefactor, "No, I don't like herrings. Take the plate away and, if you must, please offer me something else?" Of course not.

I heroically, and I do mean *heroically,* repaid all the kindness the Austrian people showed toward me. I ate the entire order of herrings, smiling and expressing gratitude, while the generous man happily acknowledged my thanks.

A couple of weeks after arriving in the refugee camp, we heard the news that in Hungary the arrests of revolutionaries had been accelerated. We knew that many of the incarcerated would never return from communist captivity. Rudi, Csaba, and I became convinced that Hungary would not gain its freedom in the near future. The time had arrived to decide in which country we wanted to live. Our long deliberations resulted in choosing Canada, whose representatives at camp promptly signed us up. I do not remember all the reasons for our choice, but I know that the deciding factor in choosing Canada was that it was a destination about which all three of us could agree. It was very difficult for us to make a decision of such magnitude in a short time, to leave for a faraway country whose language we did not speak, whose culture we were not acquainted with.

Soon after we decided to leave for the New World, the Canadian representatives offered us a trip on a luxurious ocean liner, leaving for Montreal from a French port in the middle of December. "This is fantastic!" said Csaba. "A free trip on a ship is everything we could dream of."

We had read stories about the big ocean liners and talked among ourselves about what we would experience. We were looking forward to seeing the elegant travelers dining in their tuxedos while the band played soft music. We might be able to see card sharks cheat their unsuspecting victims and gigolos look for rich widows. And there would be swimming pools, theaters, movies. What a trip, what an opportunity!

Coming from a poor communist country, the luxurious trip across the Atlantic Ocean seemed like a dream that we would not want to miss.

Unfortunately, that is exactly what we did. Rudi informed us the following day:

"I just found out that airplane tickets are available, on an earlier day. What do you think?"

It is not easy to be a refugee, even if all your needs are taken care of. Or, I should say, especially if they are. For some people it may not be burdensome to accept help, but we felt very uncomfortable about it. Free meals, free lodgings, free transportation, everything free, free, free, without giving anything in return.

Knowing what our decision would be, Csaba looked at Rudi and grumbled, "Did you have to inquire?"

Untouched by the welfare mentality, Rudi, Csaba, and I felt that flying to Canada rather than arriving there by ship would shorten our reliance on charity by a week or two. We decided to take the quickest route. I feel about that decision as I feel about my first childhood experience in a coffeehouse. I was eleven years old, on a vacation at Grandmother's in Budapest. My father had a business meeting with a client one afternoon, and he took me along. Father's client asked the waiter to bring the pastry tray for me, while they had their coffee. Drooling over the wonderful display on the tray, I selected only one pastry and refused a second helping, out of politeness. Strange, how that little episode stayed with me. I had not had my second pastry in my childhood, and as a young man I did not have my trip on an ocean liner.

In the middle of December, the time arrived to depart. A small bus took Rudi, Csaba, me, and about ten other refugees to Vienna's Airport. On the way to the airport I looked at road signs pointing toward my country, home, and family. As the airplane took off, clouds covered the view of nearby Hungary, preventing me from having a last glance at that unfortunate land. Soon the plane turned west, and I was overwhelmed with mixed feelings—feelings of great expectations for my future but also of sorrow for my country, and a degree of guilt for abandoning the struggle while others still clung to hope against hope in my hometown.

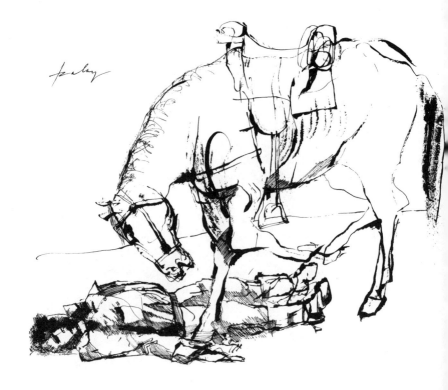

GETTING THERE

"Did you speak any English when you left Hungary?" inquired Nicholas when I told him the story of my arrival in North America.

"No, none at all."

"That must have been tough."

During my school years in Hungary, I took seventeen years of foreign languages: Latin, French, German, and Russian, but not English. Actually I knew some English, about a half dozen words, picked up from popular Western books. My English vocabulary, including words like "cowboy," "hands up," and "Winchester," nearly got me into trouble right after our arrival in the New World.

The trip from Vienna to the New World was quite circuitous. Since the free airplane tickets were issued on a standby basis, we had long waits for available seats at various airports. Zurich was our first destination, followed by Amsterdam, with a complimentary meal at the airport while waiting for a flight to Glasgow. We saw only the airports of these great cities. From Glasgow the overseas flight was heading to New York, with an unscheduled emergency stop in Gander, Newfoundland. With the modest speed of propeller planes and all the waiting at airports, the trip seemed endless. But the excitement kept us awake.

On the plane from Glasgow to New York, after a meal, the stewardess offered us a long yellowish-green fruit.

I gave her a puzzled look. She talked slowly and loudly, the way it is customary to communicate with people who do not speak one's language. "It's a *ba-na-na.*"

The word "banana" is similar in Hungarian, so I understood. I had never seen a banana before; the communists did not spend foreign currency on such luxuries, at least not for the population at large. It was no great loss for me; I never developed a liking for that fruit. Unlike when I was offered the herrings in Austria, on the plane I felt no obligation to eat what I did not want. Besides, Csaba, sitting next to me, was happy to help.

My first encounter with Americans on U.S. soil was with customs officials. Checking through our knapsacks a customs officer asked me to open the aluminum food container in which I carried my sandwiches during our escape. In Austria we were well supplied with oranges and lemons, presumably to increase our vitamin intake. In the container I had a few pieces of these fruits. I realized from his troubled expression that it was "forbidden fruit." I learned that travelers were prohibited to bring agricultural products into the country.

The officer motioned towards his supervisor, who came over. The two of them looked at the fruits, at me with my refugee appearance, and at the fruits again. Finally, glancing around, the supervisor indicated to his colleague to close the lid on the container and waved me on. Obviously, he did not have the heart to confiscate a substantial portion of my worldly possessions.

It was at New York International Airport that my knowledge of a few English words almost got me into trouble. Wanting to visit the washroom, I noticed the sign on the door: MEN. I ignored the fact that the letters W and O were in front of MEN. My exit was much faster than my entry through that door.

A taxi took Rudi, Csaba, and me to LaGuardia Airport, where we finally boarded the last plane of our trip. The exhausting journey took its toll. I slept soundly, until the plane touched down in Toronto. On that flight Csaba met a fellow Hungarian, Paul Biringer, who was sitting next to him. Paul had left Hungary before the war and was working in Toronto as a scientist. Recognizing Csaba's nationality, Paul offered his help. Later he took us out a few times to show us the sights of Toronto, and he was instrumental in channeling me in the right direction to find my first job.

12

ON TRACK

"Toronto is beautiful! We had a great time," announced Nicholas. Knowing that Ontario's capital is where I started my North American life, my boys were interested in visiting it. Nicholas finally had the opportunity to go to Toronto with a few college friends during an Easter vacation.

"Did you visit Uptown?" I asked Nicholas. "The intersection of Yonge and Bloor?"

"But of course," said Nicholas. "You asked me to."

"How was it?" I had not been in Toronto for quite a few years and was curious what impression that area of the city made.

"One of the nicest urban areas of the city," declared Nicholas, who picked up expressions like "urban area" from his city planner father.

What a change from the time I stood at the corner of Yonge and Bloor Streets with Rudi and Csaba, in December, 1956, shortly before Christmas.

Along with others in a small group of refugees, we arrived in Toronto by plane and were placed in a large rooming house earmarked for demolition. The building, located on Jarvis Street, received a stay of execution to provide temporary housing for some of the thousands of Hungarian refugees arriving in Canada. The processing of immigration papers took place in that house. After our Canadian documents were issued, the three of us went for a walk, excited and curious, to discover the country we had selected.

It was the morning rush hour, but quite different from the one in Budapest. There were hardly any pedestrians here in Toronto, but the roadways were full of huge cars, their drivers rushing to work. Arriving at the first major thoroughfare, Bloor Street, we noted red streetcars proceeding slowly, their movement hampered by the heavy automobile traffic.

In the center of the street crossing, a policeman was directing the traffic with frequent whistle blowing and exaggerated arm movements, urging the motorists to pass through the intersection as fast as they could.

"Have you guys noticed," I asked, "that this is the only policeman for as far as we can see in any direction?"

"And he is busy directing traffic," responded Csaba. "Looks like they are not afraid of civic unrest or revolutions here."

More activity was apparent to our left, so we turned in that direction, reaching the intersection of Yonge and Bloor Streets. There were more pedestrians at this location, but the vehicular traffic was still overwhelming. According to our past experience, only party dignitaries were supposed to ride in autos, and mostly in black, chauffeur-driven, Russian-made Zims. But here, it seemed, everyone was on wheels.

The prewar buildings at the intersection were of varying heights and without much aesthetic appeal. Crossing Yonge, we stood in front of a one-story men's clothing store.

"What part of Toronto do you think this is?" asked Rudi, as we tried to orient ourselves.

"Looks like the center of a suburb," I ventured. "I guess near the city center the architecture would be far more imposing and attractive."

When we found out that the area of our observation was the elegant Uptown, we got our first lesson in the difference between the Old and New World. Unlike in Budapest, the cityscape in Toronto was poor. The architecture and heights of buildings did not complement each other. No parks with sculptures or other decorative elements enhanced the major intersections. On the other hand, the interiors seemed luxurious, whether in an office or apartment building, store, or single-family house.

What a great change occurred in Toronto during the past few decades! Ontario's capital has become one of North America's prominent cities, a cultural and entertainment center with beautiful new developments, including a revitalized waterfront along Lake Ontario.

Soon after our unexpected departure from Hungary and arrival in Canada, we stood at the corner of Yonge and Bloor, realizing the finality and magnitude of our step. Less than a month earlier we had been at home, on a different continent, participating in a struggle for freedom. We had not had the opportunity to prepare ourselves for the sudden and tremendous change that would occur in our lives. The shock of the unexpected change, the fact that the location of our new home to a large extent depended on other people and circumstances beyond our control, and especially the reluctance with which we left our country had its effect on us.

We began to react with a subconscious rebellion to our forced change of life. A strong desire emerged within us to be back in Hungary so that we could help the situation there. For years, all my Hungarian friends with whom I discussed this subject had the same, constantly recurring dream as I did, always ending in a nightmare. At least once a week I woke up in a sweat after dreaming that I was back in Hungary and that the secret police would not allow me to return to freedom. My friends and I were free from these unpleasant experiences only after the communist government in Hungary allowed the former refugees to visit the country and return to the West at will.

But the recurring dreams did not affect our everyday life. Although the short stay in an Austrian refugee camp did not give us enough time to prepare for a totally different way of existence, culture, and language, we adjusted well to the new lifestyle.

I had no hope of finding work as an architect without Canadian experience and at least an elementary knowledge of English. It took a few weeks of concentrated study before I was able to carry on a limited conversation in English. Aside from personal abilities, luck, and the economy, the speed of applying one's education in a foreign land depends to a large extent on the type of education one has. Rudi, a physicist, was able to apply his knowledge almost immediately. On the other hand, our lawyer and teacher friends, for example, had great obstacles. Because the materials used and architectural details were so different in Canada, my profession fell somewhere in between as far as adaptability to the new country was concerned.

I received information about a job opening for menial work at a meat packing company on the outskirts of Toronto. I went to the advertised address. Standing in front of the large building, I became concerned. The odor of its products was apparent at least within a half mile radius. It was a tremendous relief when I did not receive an offer of employment. Had I been offered the job, I could not have refused it, although I dreaded the possibility of being inundated, day after day, with the strong smell of meat processing.

Hiring was slow during the holiday season, but soon after the New Year Paul Biringer recommended me to an engineering firm, where I landed a draftsman job. I was on the right track. I immediately moved into a furnished room in a modest area of Toronto and started saving for new clothing to camouflage my refugee status. I had escaped not only from communist oppression but also from having to accept free room and board.

Finally, I felt really free.

13

REACQUAINTED WITH PRIVATE ENTERPRISE

"Don't forget, Dad, to give him a good tip," Gordon reminded me, as we were waiting for the valet to deliver our car at the entrance of Westchester Country Club's main building. We had finished a wonderful dinner to which the boys' "adopted" American relatives, Uncle Hank and Aunt Marj, invited us.

"How could I forget?" I responded. "Special tips for valets parking cars, just as for cloakroom and elevator operators."

During his previous summer vacation Gordon was valet parking at a prestigious golf club and at one of the Hilton Hotels. Fresh out of high school, Gordon loved his job, even after crashing a Mercedes and receiving the nickname of Crash Gordon. The people he served were often generous, and now, out of solidarity, we were obligated to tip well all valets parking cars, on the rare occasions we used them.

I have similar sentiments toward cloakroom attendants because I myself was one, in my spare time, in my first years in Toronto. During days I worked as a draftsman. Three evenings a week I attended accelerated English classes at the University of Toronto made available for Hungarian refugees. On other evenings I joined my two young cousins, János and Tibor, in a restaurant where they alternated between being busboys and dishwashers. (Neither my bank vice president cousins nor I list these activities on our resumes.) János and Tibor also escaped from Hungary and immigrated to Canada a few months after I arrived there.

As a cloakroom attendant I had to place a sign on the counter demanding twenty-five cents for each item from participants at special functions. In those days that sum was outrageously high, and not everybody was willing to pay it. That fact did not bother me, since I collected a considerable amount of money anyway. On my first day on the job, my coworkers, who knew the system, told me that I was expected to give only about eight or nine dollars to the manager, who would pocket that sum. I could take the rest of the money. It was not a bad deal for us. Our earnings were off the books since the owner of the restaurant did not know about this source of income. The manager was not supposed to charge at all for cloakroom services. I was getting reacquainted with private enterprise.

During my early years of immigrant life, my friend Marci made extra money working as an elevator operator. Because we spent a lot of time together, he got me into the habit of tipping elevator operators. Since then, automation eliminated this extra expense.

As an immigrant in a rich country, I could enjoy the material advantages immediately when I started working. But I felt fulfilled in Canada only when I finally was again able to work as a professional after earning a postgraduate degree at the University of Toronto with the help of a fellowship. Meanwhile my friend Rudi Kriegler was studying for his doctorate in physics, also at the University of Toronto. A couple of years later I married a Scottish girl who came over to Canada from Aberdeen. (She *did* have her trip on an ocean liner.) Rowena planned to work in the country for only a year and then return to Scotland. We met a few days after her arrival, and that sealed our future.

A few years later a unique opportunity presented itself for a challenging job. In my last position in Canada I headed the Master Plan Section of Expo '67 in Montreal.

From Montreal, we moved to the United States, where I have been able to work on a variety of interesting and challenging projects, planning cities and land developments. However, there was at least one occasion when my work in the United States more closely resembled the kinds of jobs a new immigrant lacking any skills would perform.

I was reminded of this occasion one day when Gordon, in his early teens, came home from the library and asked me, "Dad, do you know who Bólyai was?"

"Of course. A Hungarian mathematician of the nineteenth century, from Transylvania. There is a Hungarian language university there, or rather a remaining section of that institute, named after him."

Bólyai University is the main source of higher education for the able students of about two million Hungarians living in Romania. Unfortunately, the postcommunist, extremist, "democratic" Romanian government, as part of a systematic effort, was trying to further limit Hungarian education, language, and culture, and the Western Christian religions that Hungarians practice. The Romanian version of "ethnic cleansing" was at its height under the communist dictator Nicolae Ceausescu, who in 1968 eliminated the Hungarian Autonomous Area in Transylvania. He also ordered the construction of large housing developments for Romanians around Hungarian cities, to ensure that Romanians would be in the majority. The "democratic" Romanian government followed a different tactic. They rescinded the parochial schools' right to issue diplomas. These parochial schools are educating the Hungarian population. It is ironic that these actions have been taking place in a land where, under Hungarian rule, laws were passed in 1568 and 1615 that were the first in Europe to assure freedom of worship of all religions by all nations.

"How did you come across Bólyai's name?" I asked Gordon.

"In the library. I have to do a report on the world's ten greatest mathematicians ever. Bólyai is one of them."

That information surprised even me. I knew of Bólyai but did not fully realize his importance. I was more acquainted with the achievements of recent Hungarian-American musicians, artists, and scientists. Proportionately, Hungary produced the most Nobel Prize-winning scientists, most of whom eventually ended up in the United States. But in America, when it comes to Hungary or famous Hungarian-Americans, most people remember only Gypsy music, the Rubic Cube, or goulash. But that is not always the case, as one encounter I had proved.

One Saturday morning when our children were small, my wife left early to go to a tag sale for an estate. To allow her ample time with the boys, she did not have a job for a few years. To get out of the house, have fun, and supplement my income, Rowena, a professional woman, occasionally helped a friend, Gloria Younger, to run one of her famous tag sales. Great American institutions, tag sales. They are generally conducted on a weekend, usually in a house that was recently sold because of death or retirement. The entire contents are priced in such a way that by Sunday evening everything is sold. All items must go, from expensive paintings and furniture to old lawn mowers, from television sets to bric-a-brac. Soon after she left, Rowena called. She sounded frantic.

"Csaba, we're in trouble. Can you help?"

"Help with what?"

"The man who is supposed to guard the door just canceled."

"Not exactly a high-level position," I commented. I was wondering whether it would be embarrassing if one of my clients—perhaps the mayor or a city councilman—happened to walk in while I was guarding the door, but I decided that there was nothing wrong with doing any kind of honest work.

"Just for a couple of hours, until the madhouse is over. People are already lining up at the door. There is a large yard where the boys can play."

Rowena's reference to the madhouse was appropriate. If not controlled, professional dealers and other treasure hunters would run through the door as if launching an attack. "We'll pay you," she added.

"Sure. I know I'll get rich on that."

"Please . . . "

It was not that bad. I successfully controlled the crowd, checked the contents of outgoing parcels, even helped carry a few pieces of light furniture and received a couple of tips. The rush over, I was about to leave when a lady who noticed my accent approached me.

"What country are you from?"

"Hungary."

"How long have you been in America?"

"Quite a few years." I was wondering where this conversation was leading.

"Hungarians are supposed to be quite smart." She was shaking her head, expressing disapproval. "Is this the best job you could find?" The lady's knowledge of Hungarians obviously went beyond goulash.

"Well, I am trying very hard," I answered. She did not deserve an explanation. After all, in America honest work is not something to be ashamed of. Any work, at any age, regardless of one's education or social status. Isn't that one of the things that makes this country great?

14

DISPERSED ALL OVER
THE WORLD

"I would like to marry into a big family," announced Nicholas at the age of sixteen, after acquiring his first girlfriend. "I really miss not having cousins, uncles, and aunts at holiday dinners and family gatherings." Since my wife was born in Scotland and I in Hungary, we have no relatives in the United States.

Nicholas kept probing. "How many Hungarian relatives do we have outside of Hungary?" The boys had enjoyed the company of their close relatives in Budapest a number of times, but distances made it difficult to meet members of the family who had been dispersed all over the world after the Hungarian Revolution.

In Hungary most people have relations outside the country. Since the end of World War I, about a third of Hungarians live in neighboring countries—in Slovakia, Ukraine, Romania, and Serbia. The mass exodus of refugees after the Revolution of 1956 extended the existing network of relatives in the Western world.

I started to take stock. "I have two cousins in Canada. János got married in Mexico City; Tibor wedded a French-Canadian girl, and they have three boys. Karl, another cousin, settled in Sydney and married an Australian lady."

"Yes, yes," remembered Gordon, "he is the one who can ride the bicycle backwards!" Karl made a great impression on the boys when he visited us the first time and demonstrated his tricks.

"Let me tell you about the others," I continued. "Edith lives in France. She has a son and a daughter, and five grandchildren."

These four cousins of mine escaped from communist Hungary about the same time as I did after the revolution. A fifth one, Eve, lives in Germany. She immigrated to that country legally through marriage.

During the spring of 1990, I was thinking of this conversation with my boys as the jumbo jet I was on was preparing to land at Charles de Gaulle Airport in Paris. I was heading toward Metz in eastern France, to meet Edith, the only cousin I had not seen since leaving Hungary. I was anxious to meet her entire family and see how her life turned out in France.

As soon as the plane came to a full stop, the passengers stood up impatiently, waiting to disembark. Two young college girls were discussing how they would drive their rented car in a foreign country. Their conversation reminded me of previous vacations, when I toured Europe in a Volkswagen Beetle and fought for survival amidst French and Italian drivers.

Against the advice of my travel book, I did not take the bus into Paris. Especially in rush hours, the rail transportation provides a much faster entry into the city. Leaving from the airport, the train whisked to the Gard du Nord in a few minutes. From there a couple of metro stops to the Gard du L'Est, from which station trains frequently leave for eastern France.

At the ticket window I tried to recall my French. "Metz, s'il vous plait. Premiere class." Tired and sleepy after the long overnight trip, I wanted to make sure of a good, comfortable seat. To my satisfaction, the man behind the window understood my request and pushed a ticket toward me, quoting the price.

As the train moved through the picturesque countryside, I dozed off and on and was thinking about my relatives in Hungary. The previous year I was at our old apartment to celebrate Grandmother's one hundredth birthday. All my aunts and uncles attended. Although unpleasant memories of the past were still with us, the happiness of the family reunion was heightened by the impending end of communist dictatorship.

"I can die in peace now," said Grandmother. "I saw my family one last time, and the Russians will be gone soon." She interrupted her celebration with occasional cat-naps.

My mother's two brothers were also happy. Uncle Julius could now freely talk about the horrors of his captivity in Russia, and his younger brother Uncle Karl enjoyed that he was able to retire as a school teacher.

He received amnesty for his actions during the revolution, after serving his jail sentence and working as a laborer in a coal mine for years.

Edith was not able to attend the family gathering. I was wondering how she, in her sixties, looked now. She was the daughter of the oldest of my father's four sisters; would she resemble them?

My four aunts, famous for their storytelling, often entertained each other and the entire family with yarns that got longer, funnier, and more colorful with each recital. Even if the story was a little below par they worked themselves into a frenzy and laughed until tears dropped from their eyes and everyone else was rolling with laughter.

Even when my aunts lived in different parts of the country, they somehow managed to spend their vacations together. They have always been truly devoted sisters, never making even a remotely unpleasant remark about one another. When they had all become widows, they moved into one apartment in a busy section of Budapest, entertaining each other better than any TV show would. Irén, the eldest of the sisters, died a few years ago in her late eighties. Ella (the mother of my cousins in Canada), Gizi, and Zelma (the youngest) still share living accommodations and pool their limited financial resources.

The Téglás sisters did not have an easy youth. All of them teachers, the only jobs they could obtain offered meager compensation during the depression. As a young boy, I spent a couple of vacations on the farm school where Zelma taught. In the middle of farm country the houses were scattered about a half a mile apart. There was no electricity or running water in the schoolhouse or in the attached living quarters. The closest small village, where Ella taught, was about five miles away, the distance manageable only in good weather after Zelma was able to purchase a bicycle. Fortunately, she had the opportunity to share her house with her mother and two pets, a dog called Growly and a cat, Zizi.

Summers were better, livened up by family visits. Sitting on the long, covered porch, my aunts told and retold stories into the late evenings. The tales sounded more believable in the soft light of a kerosene lamp.

Looking toward the dark countryside, we actually saw the events of the stories, made interesting by my aunts, however simple their subjects may have been. Aunt Gizi described a coronation she saw in a motion picture when projectors were hand cranked. During the coronation ceremony, in the beautiful cathedral, the archbishop is walking toward the king to place the crown on his head. At that moment the projectionist got tired and wound the film in slow motion. A new projectionist then took over and began turning the wheels with renewed energy and tremendous speed, creating a comical effect. The story became more interesting in the second telling. The archbishop's dignified slow walk became a crawl on all fours, until with a sudden burst he runs and almost trips over the steps in his great hurry. He bangs the crown on the king's head with such a force that the newly anointed ruler falls off the throne, creating havoc and laughter in the cathedral.

I do not know, and do not want to know, whether there were hand-cranked movie projectors. For me, there were. And for me, a coronation will always bring a smile and sweet memories.

During the long winter days at the farm school, Zelma had to make special efforts to keep boredom away. Wanting to learn to play the piano, but having no money for the instrument, she had a keyboard made of wood and practiced her music without sound.

Living on a farm school may have been trying for Zelma and Grandmother, but I have only good memories of the place. In those days I did not feel financially deprived just because we did not have plumbing and because meat was seldom served. There was the beauty of the wheat fields waving to the tune of the wind, the river Tisza for swimming, and a playmate, Árpád, a boy of my age, "only" a half hour away on foot. And Erzsi, the young peasant girl who cleaned the schoolhouse and, in the sanctity of the dim attic, urged me to feel her budding breasts.

The clickety-clack of the train brought me back from daydreaming. As I looked out at the French countryside, the conductor passed by. I started to exhaust my French vocabulary: "Quelle heure nous arriver in Metz, s'il vous plaît? Je dorms . . . "

He interrupted me in English. "We will be in Metz in about a half an hour. I will wake you if you fall asleep." They can be quite nice, these French people, if you make an effort to speak their language.

I had not seen Edith, not even in a photograph, for more than thirty years, but I could not have missed her, standing in front of the railroad station, a composite picture of my aunts. On a tight leash, her happy little puppy jumped up and down and barked at me in a frenzy.

Edith and her little puppy helped me to relive the storytelling experiences with my aunts. Before getting into her car, Edith vividly described how stimulated the puppy was upon seeing the crowd at the station, how she barked in excitement. At her daughter's place, where she took me first, Edith described during lunch how the dog barked at people she did not like and growled at all policemen. At dinnertime in her son's home, he was amazed to hear how viciously the little dog attacked and scared all men in uniform. The story sounded more colorful every time Edith recited it. Unfortunately, with no more people to visit that day, the puppy missed out on being described as a dangerous beast that routed France's armed forces.

In the middle of France I felt at home.

15

ON THE TIP
OF AN ICEBERG

Americans of Hungarian origin, at least those who came to this country after the revolution, are less "clannish" than some of the other immigrant groups. However, although we live as Americans, we are proud of our heritage and feel a special attachment to our Hungarian friends.

My boys have always been impressed by the fact that all my Hungarian relatives and friends achieved a very respectable status in their communities. They are doing quite well financially too, despite the hardships and difficulties they faced, arriving in foreign countries without proper preparation. Some of us had an easier transformation to a new way of life, others had greater obstacles to overcome.

Of those members of my family who left Hungary after the revolution, my cousin Edith in France was the one who had the most difficult time. She had to rely on a lot of resourcefulness, imagination, and perseverance to help her through a very tough life. She had to bring up her two children alone, under trying circumstances. Fortunately, Edith is the type who, as we say in Hungarian, could make it even on the tip of an iceberg. In America, it is expressed differently; the smart Hungarian enters the revolving door behind you but arrives before everyone else.

Edith got married and bore her two children during World War II, in Hungary. Her husband, Ted, drafted into the army during the last days of the hostilities, became a French prisoner of war. At camp, he was strongly "urged" to join the French Foreign Legion. He did, for the sake of survival, since he was forced to live on a starvation diet for many weeks.

As a young gym teacher, Ted was physically fit to survive the hardships of Africa and Vietnam without any problem. Psychologically, like some of his buddies, he was less equipped to endure the stupidity and brutality of his sergeant. One morning they found the unfortunate non-commissioned officer severely beaten up. The long investigation provided no proof, but a number of soldiers, among them Ted, were released from duty.

Upon returning to France, Ted found that the Iron Curtain separated him from his family in Hungary. As a former member of the imperialist French Foreign Legion, Ted could not risk returning to a communist country. His family was not allowed to join him in France.

Meanwhile Edith, also a gym teacher, struggled in Hungary, in the city of Debrecen, to make ends meet for her family. Wife of a capitalist, she could not get a teaching job in a school and was allowed to do only menial work. To earn extra money, she became a self-taught ballet teacher of private students. Correspondence with her husband would have been dangerous; the separation turned into a divorce, out of necessity.

Sitting in her favorite armchair, in the living room of her condominium apartment, Edith helped me piece together the events that occurred since the revolution, parts of which I had heard from my relatives in Hungary.

After the revolution, Edith planned to rejoin her husband in France and elected to escape into Yugoslavia. There, in a refugee camp, by chance she met our two cousins János and Tibor. The boys were trying to join me in Canada where I started my new life. Processing of refugees in Yugoslavia took a longer time than in Austria, so I was already working in the New World when refugees were still not sure whether Tito would allow them to proceed to the West.

The chance meeting of my relatives in a foreign land was welcomed by them. Together, it was easier to endure camp life, which was less pleasant in Yugoslavia than in democratic Austria. Lack of good food, uncertainty, and idleness weighed heavily on the refugees, who were not allowed outside the barbed wire.

Soon after her arrival in the camp, Edith took steps to improve their situation. When officials were looking for an interpreter to process the data of the refugees, she volunteered without hesitation.

"I didn't know you speak Serbian," said János with surprise.

"Of course I don't. But what do you have to know to be an interpreter in a situation like this? On the forms there will be a few simple questions like your name, address, place, and date of birth. I can learn the relevant couple of dozen words in no time."

By the time she was called upon to perform her duties as an interpreter, Edith was able to do her job well, and the little payment she received helped to supplement their diet.

Edith's son, Teddy, and daughter, Enikő, wanted to contribute to the family's well-being and often turned to trickery. Once they pretended to have a fight with each other. Teddy chased Enikő through the gate, which was guarded by soldiers of the Yugoslav army. The soldiers relaxed, seeing that only two young children were involved in the disturbance. Outside the camp, within sight of the soldiers, Enikő promptly climbed a cherry tree she and Teddy targeted long before. Having no pockets but wearing panties with elastic bands at the legs, Enikő filled her underwear with the delicious fruit. The guards saw through the ploy but had such a good laugh that the little thieves were allowed to return to camp with plenty of cherries.

Edith also solved the problem of boredom. A born teacher and performer, she mobilized the talented inhabitants of the camp and produced a show that became a great success. It was well received not only by the refugees but by the local inhabitants as well. The Hungarian ethnic population was especially touched by the performance.

Edith was kind enough to remind me that the modest amount of money I was able to send at that time from Canada also helped them to ease the hardships of camp life.

János and Tibor obtained the necessary papers to join me in Canada before Edith could leave for France. They, along with a group of about twenty, were ready to board a truck that was to transport the young men to Le Havre in France. There the refugees would board a ship and sail to Montreal.

To the great disappointment of those in the group, little Peter, a fourteen-year-old boy, was not allowed to travel with them. Peter's parents were killed during the revolution; he was looking for a new life among new friends. Being a minor and alone, his status was not clarified. He faced the danger of being sent back into a government-controlled orphanage in communist Hungary. His friends would not have that; they smuggled Peter on the truck. From then on, at every border crossing the boys performed a little diversion and managed to hide Peter among them. Unfortunately, their system broke down at Le Havre because of the alert supervision of the ship's crew.

Little Peter was left alone at the waterfront, looking sadly at this huge ship, taking away the only people he knew in a strange new land, his only friends. János and Tibor often talked about the feeling of sorrow, frustrating helplessness, and guilt they experienced looking down from the ship and seeing Peter still trying unsuccessfully to join his friends.

I often wondered what happened to little Peter. Who and what country gave him a home? How did he survive in that time of personal and national tragedy? I will never know.

Eventually, Edith and her family were also allowed to leave Yugoslavia and immigrate into France. There, Edith promptly set out to find Ted. She received the severest blow of her life when she learned that Ted, believing their separation by the Iron Curtain was permanent, married shortly before the outbreak of the Hungarian Revolution. It took some time, perseverance, and fairy-tale-like events for Edith to recover and become a successful ballet teacher.

Shortly after their arrival in France, Edith settled in Metz. Her main concern, the well-being of the children, was taken care of when an order of nuns took Enikő into a boarding school under very advantageous terms. She enjoyed the school and got into trouble only once, when she demonstrated the family's talent for the performing arts. As a good student and a beautiful young woman, Enikö was entrusted to dress as the Virgin Mary at a religious pageant. Carried away by the fact that so many good-looking young boys came to admire her, she showed a little too much flesh. At least too much for the nuns' taste.

Enikő's performance in the religious pageant reminded me of how ideas of morality have changed during this century. When I was about eleven years old, my father put me on a train to Debrecen. I went to visit his widowed sister Irén and her two daughters, the older of whom was Edith. One day, despite our protests, Aunt Irén asked Edith to take me to a museum. Along all four sides of the museum's large and impressive vestibule were sculptures, naked female figures. Edith, who was fourteen at the time, held her hands over my eyes.

"You're not allowed to see anything here," she said. Shielding my view with her hands, she walked me to another room. Adult visitors must have enjoyed the scene.

During her first months in France, just learning the language, Edith was able to get only a very low-paying job. She had financial difficulties. One afternoon she went to the cleaner and asked the clerk to have her son's trousers cleaned right away.

"We do not provide instant service, madame," protested the clerk.

"You'll have to," retorted Edith, "these are the only pair of trousers my son possesses, and he needs them tomorrow." The clerk did not have a chance to win the ensuing argument.

A customer who had listened to the conversation stopped Edith on the way out of the store and inquired about her circumstances and profession. "Are you going to be home tomorrow evening?" asked the woman. "I would like to drop in for a few minutes, if it's all right with you."

The next day a large limousine pulled up in front of Edith's apartment building. A uniformed chauffeur opened the car door for the French woman whom Edith had met the previous day. With great interest, Edith watched the happenings from the window with Teddy, who by then proudly wore his newly cleaned and pressed trousers.

After a short conversation that sounded more like an interview, the woman inquired about Edith's ballet-teaching experience, and she asked before leaving: "Would you be available Saturday afternoon?"

"Yes, of course," replied Edith, who by then suspected that something good might result from this unexpected acquaintance.

Saturday, at exactly the specified time, the limousine arrived again, but this time the woman's husband appeared at the door. After the introductions the man extended an invitation to Edith. "Would you like to accompany me to our house?"

The unexpected request did not faze Edith, and she departed with the man. At his mansion, in a large room, assembled about a dozen girls of obviously well-to-do families, dressed in ballet outfits. Their mothers provided the background.

The French woman greeted Edith warmly but with official correctness and asked her to give a ballet lesson right there and then. Edith never shied away from a challenge. In a few moments, absorbed in her work, she forgot about her halting French and took successful command of the class.

After the lesson, the hostess looked questioningly at one of the women who had been standing among the girls' mothers watching the lesson. Having received an approving nod, the hostess approached Edith.

"If it's agreeable with you, next week you will travel to Paris with this lady." She pointed at the woman who gave the approving nod. "She is a well-known ballet teacher in the capital. For a week you will work with her, to adjust your teaching to the French style."

Edith stood in total amazement, and the hostess continued. "Returning to Metz, for a year you'll have the use of this room free of charge. These students and any others you recruit will pay you the going rate. After a year you're on your own, you'll have to find a place for your school."

At this time, a minor miracle occurred. Probably for the first time in her life, Edith was speechless.

"Do you find this arrangement satisfactory?" asked the hostess.

"I guess I'd better start packing for the trip to Paris," said Edith, turning away to hide the tears of joy and gratitude. Her hosts understood and waited for a few minutes before offering refreshments to celebrate the newly founded ballet school. From that day, Edith had no more major obstacles in raising her children.

We enjoyed exchanging information about the past thirty years. It is amazing how much information can be conveyed by three people—Teddy and Enikő also joined in later—in a short time, if they are blessed with the talent of verbal communication. Edith's five grandchildren, all teenagers, even produced an impromptu concert and dance performance. There was no language problem; the grandchildren spoke pretty good Hungarian, since Edith's children's spouses were both from Transylvania.

Sadness fell upon us only when we discussed the terrible life of Hungarians in Transylvania, where under the rule of extremist Romanians the existence of over a thousand years of Hungarian culture was threatened with extinction. Since then, new elections in Romania brought into power a government that offers a glimmer of hope for improved treatment for the large Hungarian population of that country. Now Slovakia has turned to extreme treatment of the Hungarian minority. A few of the Hungarian-populated towns in that country erected small monuments in 1996 to commemorate the Hungarians' arrival into the Carpathian Basin eleven hundred years ago. So great is the hatred among the "democratic" Slovak government officials that they ordered the monuments' destruction and, as punishment for their action, levied fines on the towns.

Living in a free country, it is difficult to understand the mentality of those who in this day and age still discriminate against people based on their national origin and culture.

EPILOGUE

I am happy that my children did not have to go through the hardships my family, friends, and I experienced in my youth. On the other hand, I wish that they and others as well could gain the understanding that those experiences provided. Millions of people in the world still live under foreign rule or dictatorships or in poverty, without much hope for the freedom and opportunities that we so often take for granted. The collapse of communism in Europe improved life for many. However, in some of the so-called democracies, instead of more tolerance, minorities face increased discrimination, as recent events in Central and Eastern Europe demonstrate.

I cannot say that our family has not experienced discrimination in America because of my foreign background. Our sole confrontation happened when my boys were just a few years old. During the holiday season we visited a temporary live animal display with goats, sheep, and rabbits.

Standing beside Nicholas was a little girl about the same age as he was. Always very social, Nicholas started the conversation. "Nyuszi," he said, pointing at the rabbit. "Nyuszi" means bunny in Hungarian. Bunny rabbit was missing from my son's English vocabulary at the time.

"That's not a 'nyuszi,' that's a bunny rabbit," replied the girl, somewhat annoyed.

Nicholas shook his head. "It *is* a 'nyuszi.' A nice one."

Gordon, who could hardly speak yet, came to the support of his brother. "Nyuszi, Nyuszi" was all he managed to say, pointing emphatically at the poor rabbit, who had no idea that he had become the center of a major international controversy.

The boys' conviction produced an unexpectedly strong reaction. "It's not a 'nyuszi,' it's a bunny rabbit!" the girl screamed and ran to her mother.

"Mummy, Mummy! These boys say that that's a 'nyuszi,' and I know that it's a bunny rabbit! Isn't it?"

"Of course, it is." The mother tried to quiet her daughter. "But it's also a 'nyuszi.' Besides English, the little boys speak another language, and in that language 'nyuszi' means bunny rabbit."

"Oh!" said the little girl, apparently realizing that there was nothing devious in her adversaries' claims.

"You understand it now?" asked her mother.

"Yes, Mummy."

"Then go and tell that boy that it is both a 'nyuszi' and a bunny rabbit."

"Okay," said the little girl. Now totally calm, she walked over to Nicholas and announced with authority, "My mother said it's *not* a 'nyuszi'! It's a bunny rabbit!" She stamped her foot defiantly and turned away with an expression of majestic self-confidence.

The unyielding attitude of the little girl reminds me of countries such as Serbia, Bosnia, Romania, and Slovakia, where people still cannot accept that others who have lived there for centuries have the right to maintain their language, culture, or religion within the boundaries of their countries. The little girl has since grown up. When will the people and rulers of these countries grow up as well? Or will they create more opportunities for wars, leading to more human suffering?

This book is about my experiences and those of my family and friends. However, it is also about ethnic cleansing under fascist and communist dictatorships. Recollecting personal events in history would not be of much benefit if we did not try to learn and draw conclusions from those events. With that in mind, I'd like to add a few thoughts that are not strictly part of my story.

Both world wars erupted as the result of conflicts between ethnic groups and territorial claims either in the Balkans or in Central Europe. This fact points out the importance of ensuring conditions in that region that will eliminate the friction and hostility between different nationalities. This goal is a difficult one. The centuries-long wars with the Turks and their extended occupation caused large scale migrations, changing the ethnic composition of the countries in that region. After the First World

War, the Versailles Peace Treaty, defying President Woodrow Wilson's intentions, set most countries' boundaries in the region without considering the inhabitants' national origins. Conflicts may occur when nations that have a large number of their subjects under the control of a foreign, often hostile country wish to assure sufficient minority rights to their brethren or to unite with them. Armed conflicts can also be started by dissatisfied minorities under foreign rule. The recent war in the former Yugoslavia, especially in Bosnia, provides a prime example of nations' desires to unite and defy artificially established international borders.

The Serbs have a reasonable objective in trying to unite the Serb populated areas of Bosnia with Serbia. Unfortunately, they tried to reach this goal with inhumane methods, culminating in ethnic cleansing. Their justification for taking up arms is that while the United Nations in theory supports the self-determination of all nationalities, in practice there is no peaceful way to reach that goal. The Serbs were able to achieve closer political and cultural ties between Serbs of Serbia and Bosnia only through war.

The rest of the world observed the tragedy of the Bosnian war for a long time without effectively interfering; that inaction led to the armed conflict's widening to a larger geographical area. When Richard Holbrooke, former Assistant Secretary of State, finally negotiated the Bosnian peace treaty, he stated that the long inactivity by outside nations in the recent war in the former Yugoslavia was "the greatest collective failure of the West since the 1930s." Although NATO troops ensure peace in Bosnia, the peace treaty unfortunately does not solve the underlying problems of Bosnia or the area as a whole. The treaty forces questionable conditions on the warring parties. Rather than uniting separated portions of areas with Serb population, it demands that a large number of Serbs continue to live in Bosnia. Two peoples that at best dislike, at worst, hate each other are forced to live in the same country. Even more troublesome is the fact that while this "peace" treaty at least assures a great degree of independence to the Serb minority of Bosnia, it totally ignores the rights of other minorities in the rest of the former Yugoslavia. Those minorities did not commit ethnic cleansing, they did not commit crimes against humanity, thus they were not awarded the same rights that the Serbs were. Should not this fact also be considered a "collective failure of the West?"

Lasting peace in the region may be achieved only by satisfying the right of self-determination of all, not only those who take up arms. Are NATO and the United Nations providing lasting peace in that area, or have they sown the seeds for more armed conflicts? The peace treaty, forgetting the rights of other groups, rewarded only those who started a war and committed crimes against humanity in order to reach their goals. Under these circumstances, following the Serbs' example, will more armed conflicts and a resurgence of extreme political ideas occur to serve rightful or excessive interests of different nationalities? Can another dictator emerge, seizing the opportunity discontent can provide? Will people in the region have to continue to live in fear of war?

We should look into the past and remember the suffering that wars, dictatorships, and ethnic cleansing cause. There is a solution other than satisfying the demands of only those who are willing to deal destruction in order to reach their goals. We should not only preach self-determination but truly work toward giving those rights to people of all nationalities. Let us not risk the upheaval of another large-scale war, originating in the area of Europe where erupting conflicts inflamed the entire world in the past.

EASTERN EU   PEAN STUDIES
Stjepan G. Me   vić, Series Editor
Texas A&M   niversity Press

Cigar, Norman. *Genocide in Bosn   The Policy of "Ethnic Cleansing,"* 1995.
Cohen, Philip J. *Serbia's Secret V   Propaganda and the Deceit of History,*
  1996.
Gachechiladze, Revaz. *The Ne   eorgia: Space, Society, Politics,* 1996.
Meštrović, Stjepan G., ed. *The   nceit of Innocence: Losing the Conscience
  of the West in the War again   Bosnia,* 1997.
Polokhalo, Volodymyr, ed. *T   Political Analysis of Postcommunism: Un-
  derstanding Postcommunis   raine,* 1997.
Quinn, Frederick. *Democracy   Dawn: Notes from Poland and Points East,*
  1997.